COLLECTING AND USING PUBLIC LIBRARY STATISTICS

A How-To-Do-It Manual for Librarians

Mark Smith

HOW-TO-DO-IT MANUALS
FOR LIBRARIES

NUMBER 56

NEAL-SCHUMAN PUBLISHERS, INC.
New York, London

Published by Neal-Schuman Publishers, Inc.
100 Varick Street
New York, NY 10013

Printed and bound in the United States of America

Library of Congress Cataloging-in-Publication Data

Smith, Mark, 1956–
    Collecting and using public library statistics : a how-to-do-it
manual for librarians / Mark Smith.
        p.   cm. — (How-to-do-it manuals for libraries ; no. 56)
    Includes bibliographical references (p.) and index.
    ISBN   1-55570-206-6 (alk. paper)
    1. Public Libraries—United States.   I. Title.   II. Series.
Z669.8.S62   1995
027.473—dc20   95-36527

To Catharine and Peter

CONTENTS

FIGURES

ACKNOWLEDGMENTS

This book would not exist if Jeanette Larson, my colleague at the Texas State Library, had not suggested it and put me in contact with Neal-Schuman Publishers. John Lorenz and the U.S. National Commission for Libraries and Information Science deserve special thanks for their support in developing my manual, *Counting What You Do*, on which the concept for this book was based. Also at the Texas State Library, thanks go to Elizabeth (Bell) Clarke for all her help in understanding the intricacies of Texas public library statistics collection, to Anne Ramos, who helped with my research, and to my boss, Edward Seidenberg, who was involved in the early development of the Federal-State Cooperative System for Public Library Data and who has enthusiastically supported all aspects of my work with public library statistics.

The participants in the National Center for Education Statistics public library data collection effort, especially the members of the FSCS Steering Committee, have been vital to my understanding of public library statistics in general and the FSCS project in particular. Thanks to Keith Lance, Sandi Long, Jay Bank, Christie Koontz, Jacci Herrick, the Boulder Public Library, and the Friends of Tennessee Libraries for contributing examples of data use. For permission to reprint the definitions in Appendix B, thanks to Carrol Kindel of the National Center for Education Statistics. To Walt Terrie, thanks for taking the time to give me a Statistics 101 course in the bar of the Washington Vista Hotel.

Finally, many thanks to my wife, Catharine Wall, for her patience, encouragement, and especially her close reading and thorough editing of the manuscript.

INTRODUCTION

Much of library management is about collecting, interpreting, and presenting statistical data. Whether we call them records, files, or something else, even the smallest library takes care to track what it owns, what it spends, and how many customers use how many of its resources.

In fact, along with health care, banking, insurance, and baseball, library work must rank as one of the most records-intensive of all endeavors. With the catalog, the shelf list, bookkeeping, circulation records, patron files, turnstile counts, meeting-room logs, attendance sheets, purchase orders, invoices, payment slips, board minutes, and the auditor's report, the data-weary librarian might be forgiven for sometimes thinking the job is nothing but record keeping.

This ongoing record of the daily life of the library is collected by every employee through a variety of means ranging from hash marks drawn with the pencil stub on the back of a used catalog card to elaborate automated systems that spit out reports in endless configurations that would have been impractical, if not impossible, for even the most sophisticated library only a generation ago.

But for many library employees—especially those on the front line of service at the circulation or reference desk, as well as directors and others who must justify funding for library programs—keeping track of all of this library activity often seems like a tedious, bureaucratic burden. For many people, the very phrase "library statistics" connotes the dry, cold, analytical side of the profession—a far cry from the intellectual, humanistic realm which enticed them into the profession. This feeling is understandable, especially when the order to collect library statistics is often imposed by someone else: the library director, city manager, mayor, or the state library.

This book is primarily for the librarian who feels this way. It aims to change the way you feel about statistics by explaining why they are collected, by making them easy to collect, and by showing the value that they can have to your library. Library statistics *can* be an incredibly valuable asset to your library. Don't believe it? You will. When? The first time you convince the director to invest more heavily in your children's collection because usage is so much higher per capita in that department than in the rest of the library; or that evening when you convince the mayor and council to raise library salaries because they are 20% below those for libraries of comparable size; or the next time the local newspaper calls for information about the library and you are able to tell them that circulation per capita increased a record 15% in the last year.

But before you can accomplish any of those feats, you need to understand how statistics can help you. You should understand why you are required to collect certain data, why they are useful, and to whom. You will also have to decide what other data you need to collect and how to do it with a minimum of effort. Finally, you will need to know how to take the statistics you have collected and translate them into the most persuasive possible argument for your library.

Once you have all that down, you'll be a convert. And your library and patrons will reap the benefits.

1 WHY KEEP STATISTICS?

For many librarians and library staff the answer to this question no doubt is, "Because my boss makes me," or "Because the state library says we have to." Either of these is a valid reason, of course, but neither answers the question satisfactorily. For library data collection to be anything more than a chore, you and your staff must regard the data as meaningful. The first step in that process is to understand their importance to others and, more to the point, their importance to you and your library's users.

But you're right. The state library does want you to report on certain aspects of your library. So let's start there.

STATE AND FEDERAL DATA COLLECTION

If you work in a public library in the United States, you probably collect data because you are required to do so by your state library. Every state library in the U.S. participates in a voluntary project called the Federal-State Cooperative System for Public Library Data, or FSCS. FSCS is a relatively new program that first collected data nationally in 1988. Here's the way it works: After your state collects data from your library and all the other libraries in your state, it forwards a subset of those data to the National Center for Education Statistics (NCES), a part of the U.S. Department of Education, in Washington, D.C.

If your state is typical, only a few of the items you report to your state library each year are forwarded to the federal level. In statistical jargon, these items are called *data elements*. These few elements are extremely important because they provide a comparable set of baseline statistics for virtually every public library in the United States.

Because these data elements are collected in all fifty states and the District of Columbia, we can be certain that they are collected in your state. When discussing specific library data in later chapters, I will note which are FSCS data elements and which are not.

Your state library probably also asks you for information beyond that which is collected for the federal government. These items vary from state to state and usually ask for details about how your library operates, the funds it receives and spends, the services it offers, and how your community uses the library. Some (I hope, most) of the items requested by your state library are covered in this book. There may be others that are not. Some state libraries ask for some pretty unique items, but there is also a fairly predictable consistency about the types of information state libraries require local libraries to report.

State libraries use a number of methods to induce local libraries to file annual reports. This in itself is evidence that state library officials believe that many local libraries would not collect and report these data if not compelled to do so. State laws or administrative rules spell out the consequences of failing to report such data in most states. Such consequences usually involve a loss of either state aid, or accreditation, or both. For libraries that would not otherwise submit a report, these are usually effective. We know, however, that there are some libraries that do not report for a variety of reasons and that others report irregularly.

Filing a report is one thing, but answering all the questions in it is quite another. For this reason some states occasionally impose added requirements for certain information. Most often, these are figures that measure financial support and certain service measures.

Your first step in collecting data about your library will be to find out what your state library requires you to report. They may *request* a number of other items, but you should be familiar with what your state library *requires* and the consequences of nonresponse. Your annual report form usually comes with instructions containing detailed requirements for completion, and most state libraries will call you if they have questions about your report. If you have any doubts, be on the safe side and call a consultant at your state library to find out what you will have to submit.

A WORD ABOUT ACADEMIC LIBRARY STATISTICS

This book is mostly about using statistics in public libraries. Nevertheless, it is important to mention that the same federal agency responsible for collecting public library data—the National Center for Education Statistics—also supports academic library data collection. This program is called the Integrated Post-Secondary Educational Data Survey, or IPEDS. State libraries frequently conduct this survey, but in some states other agencies are responsible for it. These data are collected only every second year, and in most cases submission of the data is completely voluntary. For these reasons, IPEDS data are somewhat less comprehensive than the public library data collected nationally, though they are still of great value to researchers.

VOLUNTARY COLLECTION

Some libraries collect data that are not required to complete their annual report. Because data collection is time-consuming and therefore expensive, usually only larger libraries keep purely local statistics. Frequently these statistics provide library managers with detailed information about how their programs operate and how patrons use the library.

A library may, for example, track the number of reference questions asked each hour. Over time, the head of reference can use this information to determine traffic patterns at the desk and plan staff coverage accordingly.

In this example, data are collected because someone in the library—in this case the head of reference—needs them to make informed decisions. Unfortunately, this is not always the case. Sometimes data are collected because they have been collected for years and years and no one can remember why. When this situation occurs, it usually means the statistics were kept because someone asked for them: the state library or a former mayor or a library director. A way to collect the data was then devised, and staff were instructed to keep them. After a while, the state library stopped asking for them, the mayor lost an election, or the library director moved on to another library. But the library still collects them.

In Chapter 8, I will discuss how to go beyond the data you currently collect to decide what other measures you should collect. If you collect nothing more than what is on your state library annual report form, it could mean there are some areas you are neglecting. If you collect significantly more data than the state library requires, or if you do not fully understand why you are collecting some data, you might need to take another look at what data you collect and whether you really need them.

THE USES OF PUBLIC LIBRARY STATISTICS

The reason that data of any type are ever collected about any subject is that someone somewhere wants to know something. Library researchers are everywhere. Researchers in library schools use data to write dissertations and articles. In state libraries, library development staff are researchers who use data to plan statewide programs and study the progress of libraries in their states. Researchers at the federal level—in such agencies as the Department of Education and the National Commission on Libraries and Information Science (NCLIS)—use the data to study the progress of libraries nationally. Professional associations like the American Library Association continually use data to assess the status of libraries, write articles, and publicize everything from funding crises to trends in censorship. Sometimes the data you report are even used by researchers outside the library profession: demographers, sociologists, economists, and a variety of other public and private sector entities studying the impact of libraries on their communities.

All these researchers are putting your data to good use. Most of them are using library statistics to advocate increased library use and support. While these uses of library data are important and valuable, the most important potential user of library data is not in a state library, professional association, federal agency, or library school.

The most important user of your data is *you*.

So now you might be saying, "Oh, yeah, sure. I run a little library in a small town. What possible use would I have for library statistics?"

The answer is "Plenty."

USE AS A MANAGEMENT TOOL

As a library director and manager, you have a program to run. In order to run that program effectively and responsibly, you need to know how that program is performing. You need to know whether the program is successful, how people use it, or whether they use it at all. In order to answer these questions, you must have some type of library data.

"Sure," some librarians might counter, "but I can see whether we're busy or not. Statistics would only prove what I know already." Well, this may be true. Good managers tend to care enough about their programs to know how they are doing, but will everyone else? If you go to your library director and say, "Our reference department is much busier on Saturday mornings in the fall than at any other time. We need to add another staff person for those hours," what is she going to say? "Prove it." Can you prove your case for increased staffing with anything more concrete than your own observation of the reference room?

Use of statistics to support each of the following areas is discussed more fully in Chapter 9.

Planning and Role-Setting

The landmark book *Planning and Role-Setting for Public Libraries* applied the management concept known as *role-setting* to libraries. Briefly paraphrased, this means that since your library cannot be all things to all people, you must determine the most appropriate role for your library and manage accordingly. Because of the importance of statistical measurement in role-setting, a companion volume was created called *Output Measures for Public Libraries*. Together these two books describe how public libraries can go about assessing community needs, defining library service priorities, and then measuring service outputs to decide if they have achieved those goals. These works—as well as an earlier title by Ernest DeProspo, *Performance Measures for Public Libraries*—are indispensable classics in the field of librarianship and should be familiar to and used by all public librarians, especially those responsible for measuring and evaluating their libraries' performance. *Output Measures* is an exhaustive set of service output measures, their value, methods of collection, sample forms, and other pertinent information.

Statistics play an indispensable role in this process since it is through statistical measures that libraries can determine whether they are, in fact, meeting their stated goals. Also, role-setting will help you identify the types of information you want about your library and, therefore, the statistics that will be most pertinent. If, for example, your library has defined as one of its primary roles that of an information and referral center, you will have little interest in keeping detailed statistics on the use of your entertainment videos. The annual *Statistical Report*, published by the Public Library Association, collects and reports statistics from public libraries across the country. Information on libraries adopting specific roles is included.

Resource Allocation

Nearly everyone who works in a library knows—even if the general public sometimes forgets—that "free" library service is never free. In the 1980s and 1990s, many libraries have added to that knowledge the bitter truth that libraries have to compete for their very survival against other city and county departments, some of which are funded by state and federal mandate. Therefore, library managers are continually called upon to defend their programs.

Every year at budget time, the city council or the county commissioners look for ways to cut a little here and save a little there. The library director is invariably called upon to justify the library budget. At these times, it is very important to be able to make concise statements about the need for these funds. Statistics can be a very effective tool in explaining the demand for library services and the need to expand those services. Politicians will usually respond favorably to programs that can demonstrate popularity and that produce high levels of usage from a moderate investment, but they have to be convinced. Statistics can do that more powerfully than any other tool (with the possible exception of a petition of registered voters).

And just as the library director is called upon to justify a funding request against other city departments, individual programs within the library often face similar scrutiny. When dollars are scarce, it is very important to make sure that funds are spent wisely. Whether you are a library director or the manager of a department, such as reference, or cataloging, or children's services, you will want evidence that your programs are thriving under your management.

If you are the director of a smaller public library, you alone may have to determine which of your programs is the most heavily used and spend more money on those and less elsewhere. These are often hard choices to make, but they are somewhat easier if you have the data available to you to make informed decisions.

Benchmarking

In the last few years, the immense popularity of Total Quality Management has brought attention to a concept known as *benchmarking*. This means that you measure your performance in a particular area against libraries that are similar to your library. This measurement sets your benchmark. You then analyze your progress over time against your benchmark measurement. The Public Library Association's annual *Statistical Report*, mentioned earlier, is an invaluable source of information for selecting benchmark data for other libraries.

PUBLIC RELATIONS

One of the best uses made of public library data—or any data for that matter—is publicity. When a program is doing well, you want to tell the world about it. This allows you to demonstrate effective management while showing the funding authority that the library can produce robust usage with increased investment. Statistics are often the most effective way to get the word out on the success of the library. Anecdotal publicity—such as letters to the editor by satisfied patrons—are extremely valuable publicity, but they may not always be available. Statistics are a tool library staff have at hand to use to brag about the library by demonstrating its success and popularity.

By the same token, there are times when negative statistics about the library are very valuable publicity. When you must argue for a new building, it is quite helpful to show that your present facility is woefully inadequate to sustain the heavy demands placed on it.

STATISTICAL QUALITY AND COVERAGE

Regardless of the size of your library, you have one thing in common with researchers in library schools, state libraries, and professional associations. You are interested in libraries, in seeing them thrive, in directing more money to them, and in describing the good they do and the effect they have on people's lives.

Just like a well-known researcher whose picture graces the cover of *Library Journal*, the resource you will most likely use to make your case is library statistics—either yours, someone else's, or both. And like those other library researchers, when you go to build your case about the value of your library, you want to know that the data you have used are the best they can be. You want to know that librarians everywhere took the same kind of time and attention in the collection and reporting of their data that you did. You want to know that they didn't just take last year's annual report, add 5%, and drop it in the mail to the state library. Or worse yet, make up the numbers altogether.

Statisticians have a language all their own, and two of the words they use are "quality" and "coverage." Another is "census," which doesn't just mean the decennial collection of population data. A *census* is any collection of data that attempts to collect universally within a population. In our case, the population is libraries. When you submit your annual report to the state library, you are participating in a census of public libraries. The state library is trying to reach 100% of the public libraries in the state.

This is called *coverage*. Coverage is important for several reasons. If you want to know how your circulation per capita compares to the total circulation per capita for the state, you want to be sure that you are comparing yourself against every other library in the state, not just the top one hundred libraries or the few who cared to report. Coverage is also important in building a complete picture of the health of libraries nationally.

The other issue is *quality*, which should be self-explanatory. How good are the data? Were they collected or made up? Were the data sampled for or derived from an actual count? How was the sample chosen or the count derived? Are the same data collected the same way in every library? Think of the mess you would have if every library used local standards for data reporting. How valuable would comparisons be if "reference questions" meant something different in every library? How credible will your case be if it is built on unreliable numbers?

For these reasons, it becomes very important not only to use common definitions of data elements that are the same everywhere, but also to use sound methods of data collection. As I describe the areas of data collection starting in Chapter 2, I will use nationally published standards for data collection when they exist. These will usually rely upon the definitions published by the National Center for Education Statistics, which are, in turn, taken from those published in 1983 by the National Information Standards Organization. The FSCS definitions for selected public library data elements can be found in Appendix B.

Now that you are convinced of the value of statistics, let's get to work.

2 ADMINISTRATIVE INFORMATION

BUILDING THE PUBLIC LIBRARY UNIVERSE

Administrative information about your library probably doesn't seem at all like a statistic. When you think of statistics, you think of numbers. You do not usually think first of narrative information. This information about your library—names, addresses, phone numbers, hours of operation—is a very important type of data (just ask anyone who has tried to find your phone number!). Beyond that, this information is aggregated into numerical data that form something called the "universe."

Universe is a technical term that means the totality of entities comprising a set. When we speak of the public library universe, we are talking about all the public libraries in your state or, more broadly, in the United States.

We are so inundated with numbers every day that we are surprised when there are simple things we do not know. Until a couple of years ago, we did not know how many public libraries there were in the United States. Now we do. In 1993 (the latest year for which national statistics were available at this writing), there were 8,929 public library entities in the United States and a total of 16,939 service outlets. How do we know this? From the data you submitted to the state library, which was then collated by NCES to create the U.S. public library universe file. This is why we say that such information really is statistical, though it doesn't always seem to be from the local perspective. This information is then monitored from year to year so that such information as branch openings and closings, mergers, newly established libraries, and new bookmobiles is tracked.

For these reasons, your state library asks some basic questions about your library administration on its annual report form. Let's look at these one at a time.

NAME OF THE LIBRARY

Personal financial advisors will tell you that you should always write your name the same way. Choose one style for your name and stick with it. For example, don't print Jane S. Smith on your checks, open your savings account under Jane Sarah Smith, and use Jane Smith on your driver's license. This causes unnecessary identification problems and can have some unexpected—and sometimes unpleasant—results.

The same is true for identifying your library. Most likely your library has a legal name. This is usually the name by which the library was referenced in the city or county ordinance or other government action that established the library. You should find out that name and use it. This is most often a problem for libraries named after someone. How does the Groucho Marx Memorial Library in Freedonia refer to itself? As the Marx Library, the Groucho Marx Library, the Freedonia Public Library, or one of another dozen ways? For the purposes of your annual report, you should check your charter documents and select the name used therein to refer to the library. If you prefer a different name, that's fine, but inform your state library that you are changing the name of your library and then stick with it.

LIBRARY ADDRESS

Most states ask for the address of the central administrative unit. FSCS calls this the *administrative entity*. Every library in the United States is part of an administrative entity. When we say there were 8,929 public libraries in the United States in 1993, we are counting the number of administrative entities. At its simplest form, the administrative entity is a single, autonomous library operated out of a single outlet. More complicated arrangements include multiple outlets operated out of the main library, including branches and perhaps also bookmobiles. Your annual report should give you a place to report not only main library address information, but outlet addresses as well. Be sure to report the address of the central library as the administrative entity.

If your library has a mailing address in addition to a street address, be sure to provide both. Street addresses convey information that mailing addresses cannot, because they tell the physical location of a library. This can be very important in studying the distribution and use of library markets, especially where there are a number of locally autonomous municipal libraries in a closely populated area. Also, patrons may need to be able to find your library.

ZIP CODE

Your state library asks you for the full, nine-digit zip code for your library. Report it if you possibly can. If you don't know the four-digit extension for your zip code, your post office can tell you. The reason for supplying this information is that it is extremely important to a kind of research known as *mapping*. Mapping is an interesting and exciting area of computer application (often referred to as *geographical information systems*, or GIS).

These applications use data not only to make specialized maps, but also to reveal patterns and help reach conclusions about the relationships between libraries and other demographic, social, and economic factors. A more detailed discussion of GIS mapping, including sample maps created from zip code information reported by local public libraries in the United States, can be found in Chapter 11.

NAME INFORMATION

Your annual report probably asks for the names of key individuals connected with the library. At minimum this will include the director, chair of the library board, and often the president of the Friends of the Library group as well. Most states also ask for the name of the person completing the annual report form and other key staff, such as the assistant director and branch managers.

You should, of course, provide the most current information possible. This information will likely be included in any directory of libraries published by your state library. But what if this information changes after your annual report is submitted? If you submitted your report within the three months preceding the change, contact your state library to see if you can update names submitted on your annual report. There is always a gap between the submission of annual reports and publication of information contained in those reports. If at all possible, the state library will update their directory information and will be glad to hear from you.

ACCESS TO ELECTRONIC SERVICES

The rise of information in electronic formats and the tremendous potential of electronic networks to broaden the range of library resources, services, and activities have created a great deal of interest among librarians. Consequently, three data elements relating to electronically stored and networked information were added by FSCS and by 1997 will appear in the annual report you submit to your state library.

Internet Access

The first asks if the public library has access to the Internet. The *Internet* is defined as "the collection of networks that connect government, university and commercial agencies . . . and is unified by the use of a single protocol suite TCP/IP." This should be a yes-or-no question. Answer yes if your library has access to one or more Internet services such as Gopher, Telnet, File Transfer Protocol (FTP), or a community network. Answer no, however, if your library has access only to electronic mail. This question, like the others, is in the universe file because it defines a characteristic of the library and because, once answered, it will stay that way until specifically changed.

Access for Whom?

If you answer that the library does have Internet access, you will then be asked if Internet access is available to library staff only (meaning that no public access of any kind is offered), to patrons through a staff intermediary only (meaning that the public cannot access the Internet without some intercession from staff), or patrons either directly or through a staff intermediary (meaning that in some cases patrons are allowed to use the Internet unmediated).

Other Electronic Services

The third data element in this series asks if your library provides access to electronic services. Electronic services include any information service in which the information accessed by the patron is stored in an electronic format, or is searched and retrieved via electronic means. This is a very broad category of services that includes CD-ROMs, bibliographic and full-text data bases, on-line public access catalogs, and electronic document delivery services. It includes both patrons using those services in the library and those accessing the library remotely by modem from their homes and offices. Again, this will be a yes-or-no question; if your library offers any of the above services, you should respond yes.

ADMINISTRATIVE STRUCTURE QUESTIONS

There may be a number of questions on your state's annual report about the administrative structure of your library. For example, you may be asked whether your library has multiple outlets, whether it has an advisory or governing board, whether it is established as a city or county library. These are questions that only you can answer, and in some cases it may take some digging in your city or county records to find the answer. In most cases, however, they are straightforward and simple questions.

While these questions may seem bothersome, they provide very valuable information, especially to researchers studying the progress of libraries. Every public library in the United States provides these data to their state library. The state library, in turn, forwards these data to NCES in Washington, D.C. There they are collated into that *universe* file referred to at the beginning of this chapter. Sometimes referred to as the PLUS file (short for Public Libraries in the United States), this file is a data base of information about all public libraries in this country. In addition to directory information, the universe file contains codes that track many other attributes of libraries. For example, increasing formation of library districts has given rise to a great deal of current interest in the relative financial health of libraries created under different modes of establishment.

OUTLET INFORMATION

You will be asked to report on the number of outlets that your library supports. For the majority of libraries in the U.S., there will be only one outlet—the library itself. Many other libraries, however, maintain multiple outlets in the form of branches, bookmobiles, and other units. For each of the types of outlets below, you will probably be asked to report the name, address, and phone number of the outlet as well as the librarian in charge and perhaps other information as needed by your state library.

You will also be asked to provide an estimate of the population served by each outlet. While many state libraries assume the job of calculating the population served by the whole library, they cannot know the size of the population served by an outlet. Nevertheless, NCES keeps track of the population served by each outlet. You will likely be asked to say which of several population ranges the outlet is intended to target. Remember, this population is a subset of the total service area of the parent library. The ranges used by NCES are:

    1–999
    1,000–2,499
    2,500–4,999
    5,000–9,999
    10,000–24,999
    25,000–49,999
    50,000–99,999
    100,000–249,000
    250,000–499,999
    500,000 or more

NCES maintains information on two types of outlets. A *branch library* is defined by FSCS as an "auxiliary unit" of the library that has at least separate quarters, an organized collection of library materials, paid staff, and regularly scheduled hours during which it is open to the public. A *bookmobile* is defined as "a traveling branch library that consists of a truck or van carrying a collection of library materials, a paid staff, and regularly scheduled hours." For bookmobiles, you will be asked to report only the *number* of bookmobiles. Be sure, however, to report the number of bookmobiles in use and not the number of *stops* each bookmobile makes. Believe it or not, this is a common mistake!

VALUE OF THE UNIVERSE FILE

All these data about the administrative structure of the library contribute to a data base of information about public library entities that we call the universe file. All of the data described above become part of the public library universe file maintained by the NCES. This file includes other information as well, including such items as the legal basis code (municipal library, county library, multijurisdictional, etc.) and administrative structure (single, multiple outlet library, or some other configuration). In most cases, this information is reported to NCES by the state library.

This information becomes extremely valuable when researching trends in library service. How many libraries in the United States closed their doors last year? How many independent libraries merged with systems? How much of the population was served by libraries funded by cities? How many county libraries are there in the United States? Do advisory boards tend to be more common than governing boards in certain parts of the country? Are city libraries better funded than county libraries?

These are all questions that can be answered using the universe file. They are important questions about libraries that, until libraries began reporting these data, could not be known. Now the information is known, and we can provide answers to questions that have profound and far-reaching implications for the future of libraries.

3 FINANCIAL STATISTICS, PART I: INCOME

Another kind of library statistic that you might not think of as a statistic is financial information. The amount of money you receive and spend, where you receive it from, and what you spend it on tell a lot about your library. And like any other statistic, in order to be useful, it must be accurate. Let's start our discussion of financial data with income and then move to expenditures, the other side of the coin (no pun intended!).

To state the obvious, income refers to the money your library receives and expenditures are those funds which you spend. What might not be so obvious is why you have to report both income and expenditures. Shouldn't it be enough to report one or the other? After all, aren't these the same funds? To make matters worse, your state probably does not even ask that the amounts you spent and received match. If they don't even have to balance, why are you required to report both?

The reason you are asked to report both income and expenditures is that each conveys specific information about the library; they tell different stories. *Income* tells the financial health of the library, while *expenditure* measures service. The greater the income of the library, the more the program is thriving. The more money spent, the greater the level of service returned to the community. Also, knowing who funds the library provides details about patterns of local support and, in some states, can even determine who gets library service at all. Similarly, categories of expenditures tell about priorities for library service and the community's expectations of the library.

The most critical question you are asked regarding income is, "Who paid?" Most likely your state not only asks you to say how much you received, but asks for the source of the income as well. You probably have to say how much you received from local government, state and federal sources, corporate and foundation grants, donations, and other income.

To answer these questions, you will have to reconstruct your income for the preceding year. This is much easier to do if you kept track of your finances during the year. This means that you will have to set up a system to record income and expenditures. Because of centralized accounting systems that serve entire cities, many libraries—especially smaller libraries—still do not maintain their own books. A computer and an inexpensive spreadsheet program make tracking finances very simple. If you don't have a computer, old-fashioned ledger books work just fine. And while it takes a little time to set up your system, the effort will make your job easier in the long run, not just to complete the end-of-year report, but also to know where you stand at any time of the year.

LOCAL GOVERNMENT SUPPORT

The part of your income that comes from your local funding authority is known as *local government support*. Most public libraries in the United States are supported by public funds, and the vast majority of those funds are appropriated and spent by local governments. Your annual report form asks you to indicate how much income you got from what local government sources. Usually, those sources are:

- city (or municipal)
- county
- library district
- school district

Your library may receive all of its income from one of these sources, but many libraries receive funds from more than one local government source. For example, a city library will, of course, receive the majority of its funds from the city, but may also contract with the county to provide service to county residents, so that it receives county funds as well.

You probably already know about how much you received from city, county, and other local government sources. Your local bookkeeping arrangements probably require that you handle these funds separately, perhaps keeping separate bank accounts for local government funds from different sources. If this is the case, it should be relatively simple to say what you received from each local government source. If, on the other hand, you do not track these funds separately, or if you do not have ready access to information about these accounts, you will have to set up an accounting system in the library that keeps track of the sources of funds and how you spent those funds. This is particularly important if your state asks you to classify expenditures by sources of income (that is, to say how much you spent on books from local government sources).

The source and amount of local government income may have important consequences for the way in which your library is reviewed by the state library. Many states impose *maintenance-of-effort* requirements on local libraries. This means that a library has to receive or spend an amount equal to or greater than the amount spent in a previous year. In most cases, maintenance of effort pertains to local government support.

Maintenance-of-effort requirements usually work like this: Last year, the city of Littletown appropriated and spent $100,000 to run the Littletown Public Library. State law requires that this year the city of Littletown must spend *at least* $100,000 on the Littletown Public Library to "maintain effort." The consequences of failure to maintain effort may be a loss of state aid, loss of accreditation, or some other loss of benefits. In some states, a loss of local government income from one source may be offset by an increase in support from another source. In our example, Littletown appropriated only $75,000 for the library, but Jackpot County made up the difference by appropriating the remaining $25,000 from county sources. It is important that you be familiar with any maintenance-of-effort requirements in your state.

Population Served

Another reason local government income is important is that it may define the area and number of persons served by the library, a designation known as your *legal service area*. A library's service area is the set of persons served by the library. Usually the official service area of a given library is determined by the state library and is most often based upon the library's sources of local government income. If a library receives operating funds from a city, the legal service area assigned to that library by the state library will probably be the most recent census population of the city. If a library receives funding from a county, then the population of the county will likely be the service area of the library.

This can get complicated, especially in cases where there are multiple libraries in the same county or some other combination of funding patterns. A few states even assign the same population to different libraries, creating a duplicated population served. Other states have complex rules for assigning population. Texas has administrative rules governing over a dozen different population configurations. It is important that you understand how your legal service area is assigned and on what basis. The implications of the size of the library's service area may be significant. The amount of your state aid, for example, may be based on the population of your service area.

Even if your state aid does not depend on it, the size of your service area is one of your library's most vital statistics, and one that you as a manager should know off the top of your head. Why is it so important? Because as you become more interested in library statistics, you will want to know how to figure per capita statistics, and you can't figure per capita statistics without knowing the population of your legal service area. Raw data alone are useful sometimes, but in most cases, you will need per capita figures in order to compare your data with those of other libraries serving different populations. Chapter 10 contains a more lengthy discussion of how to compute and use per capita figures.

For all these reasons, it is crucial that you learn everything you can about how the state library determines your legal service area. Be aware of all state laws and administrative rules that are used to assign population figures to your library. Find out what census is being used and make it a point to know when old census numbers are superseded by new ones.

OTHER SOURCES OF INCOME

Your annual report asks you to identify other sources of income as well as local government income. Presuming that you have some type of local accounting procedure set up in your library, these funds should be easy to identify. Other sources of income may vary slightly from state to state, but will usually include the following categories.

LSCA funds

LSCA stands for Library Services and Construction Act and refers to federal funds appropriated for library purposes. These funds are administered by the state and may come to local libraries in a variety of formats. If your library was the direct recipient of any LSCA funding, the funds have probably come in the form of a competitive grant program. The terms of your grant will require that you track the handling of these funds, so you will likely keep careful tabs on the funds in your library. You do not have to worry about tracking any LSCA funds received indirectly or in the form of services from the state library, regional library system, or in some other way that is not cash. These are not income and should not be reported as such.

State Funds

You will probably have to track the receipt and expenditure of funds received from your state. These funds will usually come to the library in the form of state aid. Also included in this category would be funds received from any other state agency besides the state library. Such agencies might include historical commissions, education agencies, or agencies supporting the arts and humanities.

Federal Funds

Plan to track separately funding that comes directly from federal sources to the library. Usually this will be in the form of grant funds. You may not have to track LSCA funds that come to your library since the state library tracks this information at the state level.

Foundation and Corporate Grants

If your library was fortunate enough to receive funds from a foundation or corporate grant program, you will have to track and report these funds separately. This should be relatively easy, however, since the terms of your grant will probably require careful accounting of the funds so that you can report on their use at the end of the grant program.

Donations

You should keep separate track of funds received from donations from individuals and other local donors, such as small businesses in your community. Funds received from the Friends of the Library should be included in this category. Don't forget to count memorial donations, endowments, or other forms of donation programs initiated by the library.

Fines and Other Miscellaneous Funds

For many libraries, this category accounts for a significant portion of revenue. This category will include the following:

- overdue fines
- any fees assessed to patrons, such as fees for lost cards, nonresident fees, and fees for services
- copier receipts
- fees for lost and damaged materials
- interest received on invested funds
- income from sales of merchandise or other materials

You should only report monetary receipts. Do not, for instance, report any contributed or "in-kind" services or the value of any nonmonetary gifts or donations. Also do not report any miscellaneous income collected at the library which you must pass through to another agency (usually the funding authority) which does not ultimately come back to the library to spend.

Depending on the volume of receipts from a particular source, you may want to keep track of those receipts separately or simply lump them together. Frequently, your library board will state a preference regarding tracking these separately.

One last note of caution: Many states require that public library service be free. For this reason, they may impose regulatory limits on charges assessed by libraries. For instance, they may not allow charges for certain activities considered basic library service, such as borrowing materials or attending library programs. You should know if your state has such regulations and, if so, the penalty for noncompliance (that is, loss of state aid).

OPERATING VERSUS CAPITAL INCOME

Most states will ask that you distinguish between *operating income* and *capital income*. The difference is easily stated, but often more difficult to interpret. Operating income refers to the recurring annual income that you use to run the routine operations of the library. Capital income refers to extraordinary one-time income. Capital income is usually targeted for such major, one-time-only purchases as construction, remodeling, furniture, equipment, or for an emergency (such as repair of the building after a flood or fire).

The distinction between capital and operating income may often be blurred. Sometimes you may not be able to determine whether funds are actually dedicated to a specific purchase or not. Or, the targeted purchase may not be one of those mentioned above. The best way to determine whether funds are capital or operating income is to ask yourself the following questions:

- Were the funds earmarked for a single, major purchase?
- Is this the only year you expect to receive these funds?

If the answer to either of these questions is yes, then it is likely that the funds should be treated as capital income. If the answer to *both* is yes, then you will be very safe in reporting the income as capital income. In most cases, the state will allow local accounting practice to determine whether an item is operating or capital.

And don't make the common mistake of assuming that the only source of capital income is local government. Funds your library receives from any source, if they pass the test above, could be considered capital funds. Often, foundations or some other private donor will provide a library with funding to accomplish a single project like installing a new automation system. If your library was this fortunate, you should report the income as *capital* income from foundation sources. Similarly, if you raised funds for your new library building from local resident contributions to a fund-raising campaign, those should be reported as miscellaneous local *capital* income.

For a further discussion of capital funds as expenditures, see the section about capital outlay in the next chapter.

4 FINANCIAL STATISTICS, PART II: EXPENDITURES

Income is only one part of the picture when it comes to a library's financial data. The other—perhaps even more important—aspect of library finances is expenditure data.

Obviously, *expenditures* refers to funds that the library spends. That's where the easy part ends. Just as your state library asks you to separate your income by source, it also asks you to break out your expenditures into a variety of categories according to how the funds were spent. FSCS asks states to report separate expenditure data for the following categories:

- salary and wages expenditures
- employee benefits expenditures
- collection expenditures
- other operating expenditures
- capital outlay

Your state will separate your expenditure data into at least these five categories.

EXPENDITURE CATEGORIES

SALARY AND WAGE EXPENDITURES

These are the salaries and wages for all library staff for the fiscal year. This figure includes the salary and wage expenditures for plant operations, security, and maintenance staff, though your state may ask that wages paid to these staff be reported on a separate line then combined into one total for all staff. Longevity, bonuses, and other money paid directly to personnel should be reported here rather than with employee benefits. You should not report here any expenditures for contract labor, such as for employees provided from a temporary agency.

Salary and wage expenditures are of great interest to other librarians and researchers across the country. Many states also ask you to report the salary paid to the library director (see Chapter 7). Information on salaries and wages is among the most commonly requested. This information is used to justify salary increases for the librarians and other staff. It is quite possible that the data you report in this area will be used by other librarians in your state. This information also becomes part of a report on library salaries published each year in *Library Journal* as well as similar articles in other journals.

EMPLOYEE BENEFITS EXPENDITURES

These are the benefits outside of salaries and wages. Benefits may include some or all of the following:

- health insurance
- social security
- dental insurance
- life insurance
- workers' compensation
- disability insurance
- pension
- tuition

Report only those employee benefits paid directly from the library budget on behalf of the employee. Do not report any benefits for which the employee must pay. FSCS does not include any benefits paid indirectly outside of the library budget; however, your state may ask for this figure (see the discussion of indirect expenditures later in this chapter). Again, do not report here any direct payment to the employee, such as longevity or bonuses.

COLLECTION EXPENDITURES

These include all expenditures for materials purchased or leased for use by the public. At minimum, all states will ask for a total for all materials expenditures including print materials, microforms, and machine-readable and audiovisual materials. Your state may ask that you provide a further breakdown of expenditures by type of materials. For example, your annual report form may ask you to say how much your library spent for print materials, for audiovisual materials, and so forth. These then would be combined into a total collection expenditures amount.

Collection expenditures, like salary expenditures, are a key measure of library service. It is an example of a *service input*, or what the library puts into its service, to be distinguished from an *output measure* which refers to patron usage of the library. (Input and output measures are discussed further in Chapter 6.) While the goals and missions of libraries may differ, the amount spent on materials often says a lot about the degree to which libraries are fulfilling their role of providing materials to the public. Since many funding authorities tend to equate libraries with books, library managers sometimes find it easier to argue for increased funds for materials expenditures than for other purposes.

OTHER OPERATING EXPENDITURES

These are the rest of your operating expenditures left over after salary, benefits, and collection expenditures. It is a big lump of funds that will probably include some or all of the following:

- utilities (electric, phone, water, etc.)
- routine furniture and equipment purchase and repair
- automation costs, including consortium fees
- bindery costs
- routine maintenance of the library building(s)
- office supplies and postage
- equipment maintenance contracts

Because these costs, when taken together, produce a number that is not very helpful in analyzing trends or patterns in library spending, most states ask for some analysis of expenditures. For example, some states ask for information on repair and replacement of existing furniture and equipment. If your state does ask this, try not to confuse these routine furniture and equipment costs with those reported as capital costs. Your state may also ask you to report separately costs associated with automation such as computer hardware and software and fees for membership in consortia or networks.

EXPENDITURES FOR ELECTRONIC MATERIALS AND ACCESS

Two new data elements added by FSCS in 1995 request additional information about expenditures for materials in electronic format. These will most likely appear on your form after you have reported on the major expenditure categories discussed above.

The first asks you to report the amount of "operating expenditures for library materials in electronic format." This refers to the amount you spent for "materials considered part of the collection, whether purchased or leased, such as CD-ROMs, magnetic tapes, and magnetic discs, that are designed to be processed by computer or similar machine." The key to this definition is the phrase "considered part of the collection." This is the cost of those materials which are housed *in* the library, regardless of whether they are actually owned by the library or leased. The FSCS definition goes on to specify that you should not include expenditures for computer software when it is used only by the staff. Equipment should be reported only when the cost of an electronic information product and the machine used to access it are inseparably bundled by the vendor.

The second question asks you to report operating expenditures for electronic access. FSCS defines this as "all operating expenditures from the library budget associated with access to electronic materials and services." This is a catchall category intended to capture that part of "other expenditures" for electronic services and equipment exclusive of those for library materials in electronic format. You should include here the cost of all computer hardware, software used only by the staff, and any fees or charges associated with the access of electronic information *not* housed in the library.

CAPITAL OUTLAY

All of the categories of expenditures discussed above pertain to operating expenditures—those routine, ongoing expenditures which you expect to incur indefinitely on a regular basis. Just as there is capital income, there is also capital expenditure. These are those onetime, extraordinary costs that are incurred usually for major purchases of or additions to fixed assets. While local accounting practices will determine what is meant by a capital expenditure, the following are the most common uses of capital funds:

- building sites (real estate)
- new building construction
- expansion of an existing building
- remodeling or major repair of an existing building
- initial book stock (sometimes called an opening-day collection)
- furnishings or equipment for a new or remodeled building
- new vehicles
- major emergency repairs or other emergency costs

It may be difficult sometimes to determine whether a particular expenditure should be counted as capital outlay. Generally speaking, if the source of the funds was a special appropriation or contribution earmarked for a specific major purchase in the areas mentioned above, then the expenditure should be counted as capital outlay.

But be cautious. You may be in a state where what you report as operating versus capital income and/or expenditure has significant implications. Some states use library expenditures as the basis for determining the library's maintenance of effort for state funding or other services (discussed in Chapter 3). In these cases, the state will probably use operating rather than capital funds to determine maintenance of effort. For this reason, it is important that libraries carefully separate capital from operating income.

An example will explain why this can be important. For the previous three years, the average cost of library service in the town of Doolittle had been about $125,000 per year. Last year, the town decided to appropriate an additional $50,000 to repair the roof. In reporting their expenditures, the Doolittle Public Library reported $175,000 in library operating expenditures. This year the library has a problem. State library rules say that a library must spend at least the same amount as last year to be eligible to receive state aid. This means that the town has to spend at least $175,000 again this year (and every year from now on!) to continue to qualify for state aid. The town is not willing to increase the operating expenditures by $50,000 every year. The library is having to make a special appeal to the state library to revise the previous year's report.

State libraries tend to use operating rather than capital expenditures for determining maintenance-of-effort levels, both because operating expenditures are more stable than capital expenditures and in order to protect operating expenditures from being cut when capital projects are approved. If capital funding could be used to meet state aid, some towns would find it easy to reduce operating expenditures to pay for capital projects and still maintain local effort for state support of the library.

INDIRECT COSTS AND "IN-KIND" SERVICES

Another area of expenditures about which you may be asked to keep data and report is *indirect costs*. This term, and the practice it describes, causes library managers a huge amount of confusion (and often grief as well). This is partly because the terms are used differently in different states. What is called indirect expenditures in Texas, for example, is known as direct expenditures in Mississippi.

For the purposes of this discussion, indirect costs are defined as those costs incurred by the local funding authority (city, county, etc.) on behalf of the library but which do not come out of the library's appropriated operating expenditures. In other words, they are paid for indirectly by the funding authority instead of directly by the library.

Indirect costs may be in the form of outright expenditures. A common case of an indirect expenditure for the library occurs when the city or county pays some or all of the utility costs for the library. Another example would be when employee benefits are paid directly by the funding authority. In this case, the funding authority is making an actual cash transaction on behalf of the library. When such transactions use funds that do not come from the library's appropriated operating income, they should be considered indirect expenditures.

Indirect costs can also be in the form of what is known as *in-kind services*, those which do not involve the purchase of goods or services for the library. In-kind services are usually provided by city or county staff who do not work at the library but are doing work that supports the library along with several other departments. Examples of in-kind services commonly provided by other staff of the city or county include lawn maintenance, bookkeeping services, police and fire protection, garbage collection, and sewer services. In-kind costs often represent tangible benefits provided to the library. In some towns, however, they are used as a way to make up for a shortfall in cash support for the library. Some localities even charge the library rent on its own building!

States have devised various ways to capture information on indirect expenditures. In some states, libraries are asked to report all of their indirect expenditures; in others, only part; and in still others, only as much as is needed to maintain local financial effort for the library. Your state may also require that you provide a signed statement from a local official (such as the mayor or city manager) stating that any indirect costs claimed on your annual report are legitimate and accurate.

Whatever the case, one rule is constant: *Never report indirect costs with your library operating expenditures.* Expenditures should represent only those costs which were paid out of funds appropriated for the library. This does not mean that the city or county cannot pay your bills for you; many towns do that. But it does mean that you must report as direct operating expenditures those funds which were appropriated specifically for the operation of the library.

If you are confused about indirect expenditures—and it can be very tricky—call your state library to make sure what they want you to report.

HOW TO COLLECT EXPENDITURE DATA

Solid data on library finances are, of course, a by-product of a thorough bookkeeping system. Libraries tend to fall into two classes when it comes to financial records: those which keep their own and those which do not. If you already keep your financial records in the library, you can skip this section. All you will have to do to retrieve your financial data for your annual report, or to analyze your library's fiscal status, is extract the data from your system. Just make sure your bookkeeping system—whether it is a computer spreadsheet or good old-fashioned double-entry ledgers—is set up at the beginning of the year with all the categories of income and expenditure needed to complete your annual report as well as other data you or your library board wish to capture.

The following section is for libraries that do not keep their own books. When it comes to financial data collection, as in almost every other area of library management, you are almost always better off when you keep your financial records at the library. I can almost hear the howls of anguish from overworked librarians: "I already have too much to do. I couldn't possibly keep my own financial records!"

The prospect of setting up financial records can be daunting. There is no doubt that it is a time-consuming task, at least in the beginning. Sometimes this process means learning a whole new set of procedures—even how to use a complicated and unfamiliar computer program. Also, if you work in a city or county that handles bookkeeping centrally, they or your library board may not be willing to let the library take on this responsibility.

On the other hand, the benefits of having up-to-date information about the fiscal status of your library go far beyond being able to fill out your annual report form. You will have complete control over how your finances are tracked, what reports are generated, the status of payments to vendors, and the availability of funds. Most librarians who operate without an internal system usually find they have to work through personnel outside the library to produce the reports they need and to determine the status of available funds. This can be frustrating and needlessly complicated.

If possible, consider establishing an internal bookkeeping system for your library. This is imperative if no one else is already keeping the library's books. If someone outside the library is keeping the library's records and will not turn over that function to the library (or you do not wish them to), you should at least track key income and expenditure categories internally. Income and expenditure amounts—no matter how small—should be recorded promptly. All staff handle cash (such as fines, fees, or photocopier money) and should be familiar with how to record the receipts. A simple form or even a blank piece of paper can be used to record income at those public service desks which collect money. These should be recorded into the library's books at the close of the day or the following day to ensure consistent reporting. Again, make sure when you create your accounting system to include all the categories in which you will need to report to the state or in which you would like to begin collecting data.

The specifics of an accounting system are beyond the scope of this book. Refer instead to any of several existing books on setting up a library accounting system. I particularly recommend Alley and Cargill's *Keeping Track of What You Spend: The Librarian's Guide to Simple Bookkeeping.* Also, don't overlook the expertise of your library board when it comes to creating an accounting system. The board's treasurer, in particular, might be willing to help you. For this reason and others, it would be wise to discuss with your board your plans to set up an accounting system.

If you choose to create your own bookkeeping system, you will have to get the data off of printouts obtained from your city or county accounting department. Before the start of the fiscal year submit in writing the list of categories of income and expenditure you will need. Explain that these categories are required by the state and are needed to make management decisions about the library. Discuss with them a timetable for receiving these printouts and follow up your oral agreement with a memorandum of understanding confirming your informal arrangements.

You will probably need to receive at least monthly statements in order to prepare your financial report to the board. When you get your statements, make sure that you understand what you are looking at on the printouts. If you aren't clear about what the statement says, you will not be able to explain it to the library board or to the state when they follow up with questions. It is also important to understand accounting procedures early in the year. Do not be hesitant to ask about anything you do not understand. And do not be shy about asking that the bookkeeper make changes in procedures if the statements you receive do not provide the information you need to understand or report the library's financial situation.

COMPARING YOUR FINANCIAL DATA TO OTHER LIBRARIES

Financial data are among the most crucial tools you have for running the library. Some simple analyses of a few key financial statistics can prove to be very persuasive and powerful management tools. The power of this persuasion lies mainly in setting the data in a context that will illustrate how your library compares to other libraries. Knowing what your town spends for library service, knowing your other sources of income, and knowing how your funds are spent is quite essential. You will not understand the full significance of that information, however, until you compare it with similar data from other libraries.

Before you begin, you must ask yourself, "What do I want to know?" Are you interested, for example, in whether your library spends enough for library materials? Is the director's salary comparable to other similar libraries? Does the library spend enough on salaries? Is the city or county paying enough for the service it receives? These are all valid questions and will help define the type of data you need.

Next, you will have to pick your comparison group. This should be the group that you believe will make the most persuasive argument with your audience. One city council, for example, may want only comparisons with area libraries while another is interested in how the library compares statewide. If you think your audience is not interested in the comparison group, then pick the group that will make the most persuasive argument while being honest.

Another question to answer is whether you will be using per capita data or totals. Per capita data are totals divided by population. In picking your comparison group, however, keep in mind that for any data that can be presented on a per capita basis—such as expenditures per capita—the size of the other libraries in the comparison group is less important. Per capita figures are useful precisely *because* they equalize for differences in population. For this reason—and because they are easier to read—per capita data are usually preferable to total data, though obviously for some uses (such as director's salary), per capita comparisons will not work. (See further discussion of per capita in Chapter 10.)

Figure 4-1 is an example of a simple and effective use of financial data to make a point. This table was prepared by the director of the fictitious Jefferson Memorial Library as part of a budget presentation to his city council. The comparison group is libraries within surrounding counties.

Figure 4–1 Table Showing Use of Financial Data			
Library	**Population**	**City Income**	**City Income per Capita**
Monroe District Library	11,345	90,810	8.00
Lincoln Public Library	11,620	87,040	7.49
Adams Municipal Library	12,230	88,444	7.23
Washington County Library	13,489	96,400	7.14
Madison Free Public Library	15,275	97,757	6.39
Cleveland County Library	16,856	101,399	6.01
Jefferson Memorial Library	17,992	95,300	5.29

Note several aspects of this table. First, it uses libraries serving communities of similar size—between 11,000 and 18,000. It is a small enough set of comparison libraries to make a point, but not too few to distort the data. The table shows all the relevant data, but it is sorted in *descending* order by city income per capita. In this way, Jefferson Memorial Library is shown to have the lowest income per capita compared to all of the surrounding towns of similar size. Cities do not often enjoy the distinction of being last in any category, especially compared to other local municipalities. Wisely, the director chose to make this table straightforward. It tells a simple, eloquent tale using the most basic of library statistics.

In the next chapter we will discuss how to begin to combine other types of comparison data with financial data to give different dimensions to presentations of library data.

5 SERVICE STATISTICS, PART I: COLLECTION

You can think of library data in two major categories. The first is financial data, which we discussed in the last two chapters. The other category is library service data. Service data include those typical areas which most library employees and patrons usually associate with library work: collection, usage, and staffing. Let's start our discussion of service data with the heart of the library—the collection.

COLLECTION DATA

When the public thinks of libraries, they generally think of one thing: books. Of course, as library staff, we understand that libraries offer more than books. Most of our libraries also stock CD-ROMs, video tapes, audio tapes, compact disks, computer software, films, pamphlets, maps, microfiche, and on and on. Some libraries get truly esoteric, stocking such items as tools, toys, and sewing patterns. For convenience, statisticians use more generic terms like "items" or "materials" to describe our collections. Now, as the age of information in electronic formats has begun to overwhelm our libraries, terms like "materials" no longer accurately describe the range of resources libraries make available.

Nevertheless, though we offer more than books—a fact understood by many library patrons, too—the measurement of our collection still centers around books. And while this may change in the coming years, for now collection measurement from the federal down to the state and local level is geared toward physical items—mainly book items.

FSCS CATEGORIES

When it comes to the collection, FSCS requires very little information. First of all, they want to know only the actual number of physical items, not the number of titles. Then, they want to know only the number of books and serials, audio and video materials, and films. Your state probably requires more information about your collection. You may be required to report titles as well as items, or you may be asked to break down your collection into more categories of formats (adding, for example, microfilms, compact disks, or videocassettes). But let's start with the categories required by FSCS.

What Is a Book?

And you thought you knew the answer to this question. You probably do, but let's just state it for the record. According to the definition adopted by FSCS and, in turn, every state in the country, a *book is* a "non-periodical printed publication bound in hard or soft covers, or in loose-leaf format." It is likely that your state has adopted a definition of the book very similar, if not identical, to this definition.

Serials

FSCS states that *serials* are "publications issued in successive parts, usually at regular intervals, and as a rule, intended to be continued indefinitely. Serials include periodicals (magazines), newspapers, annuals (reports, yearbooks, etc.), memoirs, proceedings, and transactions of societies. Except for the current volume, count unbound serials when the library has at least half of the issues in a publisher's volume." In other words, count each bound volume of a serial as one item; then, if you have more than half the issues of a publisher's volume in unbound copies, count each publisher's volume as one volume. Your state may require that you report book and serial volumes separately, but in reporting to FSCS, these figures get combined into one number.

Audio Materials

This is a generic term for "materials on which sounds (only) are stored (recorded) and that can be reproduced (played back) mechanically or electronically, or both." Report CDs, tapes, and records in this category. If your library collects media kits, and your state does not require that they be reported as a separate category, they can be recorded either here or with book volumes, but not both.

Videocassettes

Videocassettes are "materials on which pictures are recorded, with or without sound. Electronic playback reproduces pictures, with or without sound, using a television receiver or monitor." Everyone knows what a videocassette is. The problem in reporting them is that they are uncataloged in so many libraries that they often do not show up in the count of cataloged materials. We will discuss cataloged versus uncataloged items later in this chapter.

Materials in Electronic Format

This is a new data element to be required from the federal level. It asks that you report the number of physical units in your collection that are in electronic format. In your library this will probably be CD-ROMs or computer disks, but it can also include magnetic tapes and other formats. You should count and report each physical unit, so that you would count each CD or each floppy disk in a multiple-disk set. You should not count individual files on a disk or any software that is used only by the staff.

EVERYTHING ELSE

Obviously, there are many other types of items in the library. You know this and your state knows this, and in most states you will have to report more than just the categories required by FSCS. Let's look at a few of the major categories not required by FSCS but often collected by state libraries.

Government Documents

Usually, a *government document* is defined as any publication in book, serial, or other format that is published by a government agency. Note that this definition does not distinguish between levels of government. Unless your state instructs otherwise, federal, state, and local documents in your collection should all be considered government documents. Usually, when states require libraries to report government documents, they are referring to a collection of materials cataloged and shelved separately. Otherwise, these materials would simply be reported with books. In this situation it would not be necessary to try to count government documents (such as the *Statistical Abstract of the United States*) that might be cataloged and shelved with other materials.

Microforms

Microforms is a generic term covering a variety of formats which store a photographic reproduction reduced in size. Microforms include microfiche and microfilm as well as less common formats, such as aperture cards, ultrafiche, and reproductions on opaque material. Microforms cannot be used without special magnifying equipment, such as microfiche or film readers. The hard part about reporting these materials comes in defining a "volume" or "item." In some states, each physical unit is reported as a volume; in others, volumes correspond to publishers' volumes. An error in counting these materials—especially microfiche—can cause a radical distortion of your collection size.

CD-ROM

CD-ROM is an abbreviation for *Compact Disk–Read Only Memory*. These compact disks contain electronically stored machine-readable data. Examples of informational materials which your library might have in CD-ROM format include bibliographic data bases, encyclopedias and other reference books, periodical data bases, census data, and telephone directories. Since FSCS asks for audio materials in a separate category, it is unlikely that your state wants you to include your music CDs under this category, but if you are unsure, check your instructions carefully or call your state library.

Machine-Readable Materials

Check with your state library to find out exactly what should be reported in this category. Usually, this will include any data files or microcomputer applications software available for public use. Machine-readable data files are data files that exist in such media as punched cards, paper tape, magnetic tape and disks, digital videodisks, and compact disks designed to be processed by a computer or other machine. This is a broader category than CD-ROM, so unless your state asks for CD-ROMs to be reported separately, they should be included here.

Other Materials

Apart from the types of materials already mentioned, libraries collect in a variety of unusual formats. It is unlikely that your state will ask you to report any of these formats, but if you are asked to report "other materials," you should plan to report any item held by the library to which the public has access. These will include pamphlets, realia, photographs, slides, toys, maps, artwork, sculptures, games, tools, sewing patterns—and just about anything else you could possibly imagine. As long as it's a library resource for public use, it should be reported here.

Subscriptions

Libraries are often asked how many subscriptions they have, but because subscriptions are treated differently than materials, they are often misunderstood. A *subscription* is an arrangement by which a library—or someone else on behalf of the library—contracts to receive all issues of a regularly published material for the period of the subscription. Duplicate subscriptions should each be counted. Subscriptions should be counted only when they are current. When you stop receiving the magazine regularly, it should no longer be counted as a subscription, but will continue to be reported as an item held by the library. Subscriptions paid by someone else—the Friends or an individual donor, for example—should also be reported. If an individual donates copies of a periodical to the library with such regularity that the library counts on receiving it, it should probably also be counted.

METHODS OF COUNTING YOUR COLLECTION

If you work in a library that has an automated circulation system, it should be very easy to count your collection. Most commercial library automation software will generate reports on the number of items in various categories. These reports can usually be configured to give counts by type of material, material class (that is, juvenile or adult), call number, or other attribute of the material. If your library is already automated and you are unsure of which of these features are available, ask your vendor or consult your documentation for more information. If you are in the process of selecting an automation vendor, be sure to include report-writing features with other specifications you expect in your new system. Report generation is a standard feature offered by most vendors, but if you neglect to ask for it before you sign the contract, you may find that the vendor will charge you extra for the feature. Or you may find that the software cannot generate a report that contains the information in the formats or categories that you need to complete your annual report or for your other uses.

The quality of the report that you generate from your automated system will be only as good as the quality of the data you maintain. Computer people have an appropriate acronym for this—GIGO—which stands for "garbage in, garbage out." Like a card catalog, you will have to maintain your bibliographic data base regularly so that it reflects the current status of your collection. It should be obvious that items that are withdrawn, lost, or stolen from the collection should be deleted from the data base just as new items are added. Aside from giving you more accurate report data, it will make your patrons happier, too.

SAMPLING FOR COLLECTION SIZE

If you do not have an automated circulation system, you will have to take a manual approach to collecting information on your collection size. You could, of course, count every item in the collection. While conducting a periodic inventory of the entire collection is not such a bad idea (and is often required in school libraries), doing this more often than very occasionally is beyond the capability of most public libraries. An inventory means not only counting the entire collection on the shelf, it also means counting what is out in circulation, determining which overdue materials are lost, and other factors.

The next best thing to a full count of the collection is a valid, thorough sampling. *Sampling* is a statistical term that means that you measure a small part of an entity and then extrapolate—or estimate—a total for the entire entity. National opinion polls are a good example of sampling. Proven statistical methods are used to select a representative sample group. That sample group is questioned, and the results are then said to represent the views of the entire population, with a quantifiable margin of error.

In a similar way, you can sample for your collection size. In sampling to determine your collection size, it is best to work from your shelflist. If your library does not maintain a shelflist, you can work from the title catalog, but it is much less satisfactory because the title catalog contains cards for added title entries and series entries.

To estimate your collection size from the shelflist, follow these steps:

1. Press the shelflist cards tightly together and measure the total number of inches of cards in the shelflist.
2. Using the same amount of pressure, measure one inch of cards in the shelflist. Count the number of volumes in the collection represented by that inch. Take care to measure and count accurately, making sure that you count multiple volumes on a single card.
3. Repeat step 2 at regular intervals (for example, count one inch in every foot, three feet, or other preestablished interval) until you have measured at least seven sample inches at various places in the shelflist. The more samples you take, the more accurate your estimate will be.
4. Average the number of titles per inch in the samples. If any sample varies from the average by more than four cards, repeat steps 1 through 4, uniformly applying pressure to the cards.
5. Multiply the average number of titles per inch by the total number of inches of cards in the shelflist.

The drawback to this method is that it does not allow for materials that have been lost if the cards have not been pulled from the shelflist. To adjust for lost materials, judge how many materials are missing from a random sample of the shelflist or catalog against the shelf and circulation records. Take at random a number of items shown in the catalog or shelflist for one area of the library (fiction, nonfiction, children's picture books, etc.). Locate these items either on the shelf, among the currently circulating items, or among items waiting to be reshelved. Any item which you cannot account for should be considered lost. Estimate a percentage of the total collection lost based on the sample.

ESTIMATING FROM THE SHELF

Just as you can derive a total by sampling the shelflist, you can also estimate the total size of the collection from a sample of items on the shelf. To derive such an estimate, use the following method:

1. In one particular area of the collection (fiction, nonfiction, picture books, etc.), count the number of items on at least five shelves (the more shelves sampled, the more reliable the final estimate will be).
2. Divide the total number of items on those shelves by the number of shelves counted.
3. Count the number of shelves in that area of the collection.
4. Multiply the number of shelves in that section by the average number of items per shelf in that area of the collection.
5. Estimate the number of that type of item checked out by counting the number of book cards. Add this total to the estimated count.
6. Repeat this process for other types of items in the collection.

KEEPING THE INFORMATION CURRENT

Once you have established a count of the number of items in your collection—either by sampling or by actual count—you will need to keep that information up-to-date. You need not sample every year as long as you take care to record additions to and deletions from the collection. A form can be easily developed to help with this process. Remember to:

1. Keep track of items that are weeded, removed, or lost from the collection as well as new materials added to the collection.

2. Centralize the tallying of these statistics as much as possible.
3. Standardize the process as much as possible. Make sure everyone who records additions to and deletions from the collection is counting them in the same way. Also be sure they are counting them at the same time in the addition and withdrawal process so that they do not double-count.

TITLES VERSUS VOLUMES

Some states require public libraries to report titles as well as physical volumes. This distinction is sometimes not so easy. Obviously, if you have only one copy of a book, then you would report one volume and one title. It's also easy to report if you have three identical copies of the same book; you have one title and three volumes. And multivolume reference sets are not too much bother, either: if you have a twenty-volume encyclopedia, you have one title and twenty volumes.

But what do you do with different editions of the same title? Or what if you have one copy of *Gulliver's Travels* in the adult section and an identical copy in the children's room with a different call number? What if you have copies that look the same but have different pagination? And what do you do about different formats, such as books on cassette? In these cases, deciding when to count a title and when to count a volume becomes more difficult.

If your state publishes a specific requirement in this area, you should follow that. If not, you can use the following rule of thumb: If you treat them as separate titles in your catalog and shelflist, then report them as separate volumes. Conversely, if you can use the same bibliographic record to describe multiple physical items, then you should treat them as one title and multiple volumes.

For example, your collection contains five copies of *The Scarlet Letter*. These copies are: two hardcovers, a paperback, an abridged juvenile edition, and a large-print edition. If the paperback is the same edition as the hardcover (same date of publication, number of pages, publisher, etc.), then report the two hardcovers and the paperback as three volumes and one title. The same cataloging record cannot be used to describe the juvenile and large-print editions. Therefore, record them as two volumes and two titles.

If you have never kept accurate records on the breakdown between volumes and titles, there is no easy formula to use to estimate. The proportion of duplicate titles in a collection is a matter of an individual library's collection development and acquisition philosophies, policies, and practices.

Because smaller libraries typically buy one copy of most items, their volume and title counts will usually be about the same. Larger libraries and libraries that specialize in popular adult reading may buy multiple copies of new titles. For a large system with many branches, the number of volumes may be much higher—in some cases 40% higher—than the number of titles.

CATALOGED VERSUS UNCATALOGED

If your library is like most, you probably have a number of items that are uncataloged. Usually these are either pamphlets or other ephemeral materials, audiovisual materials (such as videocassettes), or paperback materials. In counting your collection, you may wonder whether they should be counted or not. This will depend on your state's requirements. Some states do not distinguish between cataloged and uncataloged. Others ask that you report only a portion of these items or none at all. If you are unsure, call your state library. If your state library does not care and you are still in the dark, I recommend adopting the following rule of thumb: Count them if you consider them a permanent part of your collection. One way to decide is to ask yourself, Do you make patrons check them out and do you send overdue notices for them? If yes, then you should count them and report them as part of your collection. This will usually mean that your collection of videocassettes—whether or not they are cataloged—will be reported. On the other hand, the paperbacks on your swap rack will probably not get reported.

COUNTING WHAT YOU DON'T OWN

This may seem paradoxical. Why would you worry about reporting as part of your collection something that you do not own? Well, the good news is that you don't have to—not yet anyway. But you may have to someday.

The nature of library work has been radically transformed by the rise of such information networks as the Internet. Internet-based information sources have made it possible for even the smallest and most isolated libraries to offer their patrons access to resources they would not otherwise receive. Unfortunately, this enrichment of service offered patrons is in no way reflected in the traditional way we measure resources offered—namely, number of items.

To use an Information Age buzzword, these are *virtual* materials, resources that exist not as books on your shelf but as digital files on a computer, across the country or across the world. Your patron does not care whether you own the item but whether you can provide the information needed. Access to networked resources allows libraries to provide access to a broader range of resources, but they do not show up as part of the item count. Ironically, in many libraries they have begun to displace traditional print-based resources that can be counted in the ways described in this chapter. Because of this, one of the key vital statistics used to measure the health of a library—the size of its book stock—will likely become increasingly irrelevant and misleading.

SERVICE STATISTICS, PART II: OUTPUTS

Up to this point, we have talked exclusively about counting what you put into the library: the money you receive and spend for the library and the collection you provide for library patrons. The term used to describe what goes into providing library service is *input measures*. Other input measures besides money and collection include staffing, hours, and number of programs presented. Until the late 1960s, library managers mainly considered input measures when discussing service quality. At that time, however, some library leaders began to reorient library management theory toward the importance of measuring library usage. Their idea was that we can tell whether a library is successful in serving its clientele by measuring the amount of services used by that clientele. The more people used the library, the theory goes, the more successful the program. The term used to describe the extent of use of library services is *output measures*.

The popularity of this concept was cemented with the American Library Association's publication of two books: *Planning and Role-Setting for Public Libraries* and *Output Measures for Public Libraries*. Together, these books guide librarians in defining a role and mission for the library, setting goals to achieve that mission, and picking statistical means—appropriate output measures—though which to judge progress toward those goals.

So what are these output measures? They center around such common library practices as circulation, reference, program attendance, and visits. These statistics are often also known as *service outputs*. These measures define the core elements that most libraries use to determine the effectiveness of the library in meeting the needs of its clientele. Output measures include usage (circulation, visits, in-library use, etc.), materials availability measures (fill rates), reference completion rates, percent of population registered, turnover rate, and several other measures.

This chapter will discuss several key service outputs (most of which are probably required by your state), why they are important, and how they should be measured.

CIRCULATION

Circulation has been the flagship library statistic for decades. It is the most commonly accepted, easily understood, and arguably the most consistently and universally collected library statistic. For these reasons, circulation is perhaps the most reliable output measure of public library work.

CIRCULATION DEFINED

Circulation refers to the number of materials borrowed from the library by the public. Most public libraries define circulation as the act of lending an item for use outside the library, though there are some cases where usage within the library is considered a circulation. To be considered a circulation, the item must be charged to a patron, through either a manual or an automated system, so that for the period of the loan responsibility for the item has changed hands from the library to the patron. Renewals are always counted as additional circulations, as are interlibrary loan items that you have received from another library and then loaned to a patron.

You should not include with circulation any loan to another library or a loan to another department within the library, such as the bookmobile, the bindery, or the depository. In most cases you would also not count patron use of materials in the library. The only exception to in-library use would be in the case of a library that did not allow materials to leave the premises and which actually charged materials to the patron for use on the library premises.

Since 1993, circulation of juvenile materials has been a separate FSCS data element. This is defined as the number of juvenile materials checked out by any patron, *not* as the number of materials checked out by juveniles. Your state, then, will likely ask you to report both total circulation and juvenile circulation. It is also possible that your state or your library collects more detailed information on your library's circulation. Many states ask that you report circulation statistics by material class (for example, to report book circulation separately from audiovisual circulation).

Many libraries keep more detailed circulation statistics than they are required to report. Libraries will frequently keep statistics on the circulation of fiction, nonfiction, and children's fiction, nonfiction, and picture books. Some libraries even track circulation by call number. These libraries find this level of detail an important way of assessing their patrons' needs. By allocating collection development funds to building high circulating parts of the collection, these libraries can maximize limited funds and bring their patrons the materials they need. If the only figure collected is total library circulation, you will not know which parts of the collection are most active, what your patrons are using your library for, and where to spend your funds to the best effect.

COLLECTING CIRCULATION STATISTICS

If you use an automated circulation system, collecting circulation statistics should be relatively simple. If you have an automated system in place, you are probably already familiar with the circulation reports your system can generate. If not, you can consult your documentation and your vendor representative about how to create these reports. If you do not yet have an automated system, be sure to include report-writing capabilities in your specifications for a new system. When writing such specifications, keep in mind the categories in which you will want circulation reports. If you are not sure which categories you will want, be liberal in your specifications. The system's capability to generate daily reports is also important. When it comes time to analyze use patterns in your circulation data, the more frequent and more detailed your reports are, the more helpful they will be.

If you do not have and are not considering acquiring an automated circulation system, you will have to continue recording circulation by hand based on your manual circulation system. Most nonautomated public libraries use some form of a date-stamped-card system to handle circulation. In this system, of course, you simply count the number of cards used each day and record that number. Some libraries will count cards hourly for more frequent circulation information. If you are recording your circulation by counting transaction cards, it is important to have a system where you do not lose records. I think the most successful system is to have either a spiral-bound notebook at the desk or a daily form. At the end of each week, record the daily statistics in a ledger book, computer spreadsheet, or some other tabular form where you can keep running totals of the daily, weekly, and monthly circulation. Library supply companies (such as Gaylord and Highsmith) carry ledger books specifically designed to do this. In this way you can be sure you never lose a day of circulation.

REFERENCE

If circulation is the best understood and most reliable library statistic, reference has to be one of the most unreliable and unevenly collected. This is not only because it is often hard to tell what a reference question is, but also because of widespread, fundamental misunderstanding about the reference function itself.

REFERENCE DEFINED

Your state report very likely asks you to report reference transactions received. The official definition of a *reference transaction* used by FSCS is "an information contact which involves the knowledge, use, recommendations, interpretation, or instruction in the use of one or more information sources by a member of the library staff." Note that this definition does not ask you to report the number of reference questions answered. It is the number questions *received* by library staff, regardless of the final outcome. Also, this definition does not specify which staff member receives the question. Some libraries may report only those questions received at the reference desk. Note also that it defines *reference* as a process mediated by staff, so that any unmediated use of the library's collection or services by the public does not count as a reference transaction.

What qualifies as an "information source" or an "information contact"? The definition goes on to specify that the term includes information and referral service. Information and referral is a specialized service in which patrons are referred to agencies outside the library, usually community service agencies. The definition further states that "information sources include printed and non-printed materials, machine-readable databases, catalogs and other holdings records, and, through communication or referral, other libraries and institutions and people inside and outside the library." Note that the writers of this definition went to great lengths to make sure we understand that the term is completely independent of format. According to this definition, nearly any material with any level of informational content in your collection conforms to the definition of an information source. Between these two parts of the definition, we have a situation where nearly any staff use of any material in the library on behalf of the patron should be recorded as a reference transaction.

WHAT'S NOT INCLUDED IN REFERENCE

Anyone who has worked a public service desk in a library for more than a few minutes knows that library users ask for all kinds of information. Many of these questions meet the definition of a reference question, but many do not. Directional questions and policy questions should not be considered reference questions. The definition used by FSCS and adopted verbatim by many states carries an explanatory note that is very specific about the kinds of questions that should not be reported as reference.

On its surface, the term *directional questions* ought to be self-explanatory. By this we mean directing a patron to some part or feature of the library. The classic example is, "Where is the bathroom?" But directional questions can also pertain to situations in which it might be said that the library staff is exercising a knowledge of the collection as in, "Where are the books by William Faulkner?" In this case, if the response is to point and say, "With the *F*s in the fiction stacks over there," this is clearly a directional question. If, however, the response is to take the patron to the card catalog, help her locate a call number, then show her how to use the call number to locate the material, this more complex interaction—which involves a level of instruction in information resources in the library (that is, the catalog)—should be counted as a reference question.

Policy questions refer to any question from a patron about the library itself. Examples would include questions about hours of operation, overdue and fines policies, schedules of library programs, and floor plans. Policy questions are not counted as reference transactions.

HOW TO COLLECT REFERENCE STATISTICS

Unfortunately, there is no automated way to collect reference statistics. You must tally the number of requests by hand. Most libraries have developed their own system to record reference transactions. These systems can be simple or elaborate or fall somewhere between the two extremes. Some libraries use only hash marks on a notepad while others record hatch marks on a form divided by the hour so they can identify peak usage times. Still others have developed systems in which each reference question is recorded on its own form with information to be completed by staff on time received, sources consulted, and the final disposition of the question. Such forms—while time-consuming to complete, file, and analyze—can provide a wealth of information on the reference function, the adequacy of the collection to satisfy customer needs, and the strengths and weaknesses of the staff.

Five Popular Misconceptions About Reference

1. ***Reference equals research.*** Many librarians, especially in smaller libraries, believe that reference is the same as in-depth research. According to this interpretation, informational questions requiring short answers (called ready reference in some libraries) are not true reference (research) questions and should not be reported. All nondirectional, non-library-policy information questions should be recorded as reference transactions regardless of the length of the research time or the answer.

2. ***Ten questions from one patron should be counted as one question.*** Some libraries have adopted the erroneous practice of recording reference transactions on a per-patron basis. Reference transactions should be recorded based on discrete questions. If one patron asks for information on ten different subjects, record it as ten questions.

3. ***Only questions answered by a reference librarian (or at the reference desk) can be considered reference questions.*** False. Any informational question from a patron that meets the test of a reference contact should be counted regardless of which staff member handled the transaction or where it was asked or answered.

4. ***Count a separate reference transaction for each resource consulted in answering an information question.*** According to this logic, if you have to look in five books and three magazines before you find the answer, you would record eight reference transactions. This is clearly false. The number of sources consulted has no bearing on the number of transactions.

5. ***"We don't do reference."*** Either because they are not equipped to answer in-depth research questions (see # 1), or because they do not have a "reference librarian" (see # 3), whole departments or whole libraries sometimes believe that they cannot be doing reference. Because the public has learned to equate the library with information, it is very unlikely that any library does not receive at least a minimal number of reference questions.

Appendix A contains sample forms that can be used by libraries for recording reference transactions. Whatever method you use to record reference transactions, be sure that all staff members are trained to recognize a reference question when they get one as well as how to record it.

USES OF REFERENCE STATISTICS

The value of your reference data in analyzing and evaluating use of your library will depend on the level of detail you have collected. If what you have collected are cumulative monthly totals of number of reference questions, you will be able to compare demand for reference services in your library to that in other libraries and to state or national averages. This information is valuable, but limited. More informative conclusions require more detailed data collection. For example, if you have collected reference transactions by hour, you have collected information about usage patterns that can be used to make staffing decisions. In a larger library with multiple public service desks, this data will allow you to maximize staff placement and perhaps even the location of your public desks. If you collect data on the subject area of requests, you will generate data that, coupled with success and fill rates, will enable you to make informed collection development decisions.

In analyzing reference data, also keep in mind that what you collect will determine what you know about the data. The less detailed your data collection, the less hard information you have and the more open it is to conjecture. For example, high or low number of requests tells you only how many times people have thought to ask your library for information. Anything else is conjecture. You do not know what percentage of those requests were filled, although high reference usage might indicate a high degree of satisfaction. If usage is low, you don't know whether that is the result of lowered expectations because of patron dissatisfaction, limited hours of access, the shrinking budget for materials, or the community's information needs.

Since reference—perhaps more than other library services—is a mix of staff, collections, and patron expectations, and because it is so central to the information function of the library, it is likely that the more you know about reference use in your library, the more you will want to know.

LIBRARY VISITS

Counting statistics on the number of people who walk into the library (also known as attendance, or turnstile count) ought to be one of the most widely collected and easily understood service measures. This would surely be the case if libraries were actually run like businesses, as is so often urged in the professional literature. Successful businesses keep track of the number of customers who walk through their front doors. Unfortunately, *library visits* is a poorly understood and frequently undercollected measure.

DEFINITION OF VISITS

Because this is an FSCS data element, there is a nationally applied definition. The definition states that *visits* is the "total number of persons entering the library for whatever purposes during the year." While this definition sounds straightforward, confusion persists. One source of this confusion is that in most states statistics on *program attendance* are also collected. This can be particularly confusing in those states which follow the federal lead in referring to library visits as "attendance." Some library staff seem to think that a person entering the library only to attend a library program should only be counted as attending the program. This is false. For example, if the day-care center across the street from the library brings fifteen children to attend a story hour every Thursday and they leave immediately after the program, you should count fifteen persons entering the building *and* fifteen persons attending a program. Because this is a juvenile program, you also report them as persons attending a juvenile program (see the section on program attendance later in this chapter).

There is also some general misunderstanding about what constitutes a visit. Some library staff cannot bring themselves to report every person who walks through the front door. If the UPS delivery person drops off a package at the circulation desk, do you count one visit? According to the standard national definition you should, but many libraries do not feel comfortable recording as visits persons entering for clearly nonlibrary purposes. *Visits* refers to persons entering the library for any reason, even if it is only to use the restroom.

Another source of confusion is successive visits by the same person, especially in quick succession. Library staffs tend to count only the initial visit of the same individual in the same day. For example, if a patron enters the building, then remembers something in the car, exits, then reenters the library five minutes later, staff may not count the second time the patron enters the building as a visit. Again, the FSCS definition (probably the same as or similar to the one in use in your state) makes no distinction about multiple visits by the same person, even in quick succession. If a person walks in and out and in again, it should be recorded as two visits. Some states require that libraries exclude from the count of visitors those persons who enter the library to make deliveries, repairs, or for some similar purpose.

HOW TO COLLECT DATA ON VISITS

The easiest and most reliable way to collect data on visits is with a device known generically as a "patron counter." This is a sensing device that is installed at the front door that automatically counts each person who enters the library. Patron counters are sold by several library suppliers for around $200, a bargain when you consider the work they save and the accuracy of the data they capture. Automatic patron counters avoid many of the pitfalls that come with confusion about whom to count. Because they log everyone who walks through the door regardless of purpose, their count will always conform to the national definition. And don't be surprised if the count is far higher than you recorded manually. Between lapses in counting and intentional noncounting, a manually collected figure is almost certainly much lower than the actual number of persons entering the building.

If you cannot afford a patron counter, you will have to have your staff count patrons as they enter the library. This can be done either by actual count or by sampling (see discussion of sampling in Chapter 5). If sampling is used, a weeklong count of patrons entering the building should be conducted at least twice a year. The most frequently recommended periods for sampling are typical weeks in April and October. Observation indicates that these months tend to be moderately high traffic months in public libraries. This may not be true in your library, so you must decide what periods to sample. Take care not to pick either your busiest or your slowest months to conduct your sample—after all, you want the sample to be the best possible indication of actual usage. Because more frequent sampling will yield a more accurate estimate, sampling even more frequently than twice a year is recommended. Just remember that to arrive at an annual total, you must multiply by the right factor. If you sample once a year, multiply by 52; twice a year, multiply by 26; and so forth.

Be sure that the staff counting persons entering the building are counting accurately and thoroughly. Keep in mind that at peak times, when the highest number of persons are entering the building, staff are also busiest and thus are the least likely to have the time and the presence of mind to stop and record patrons as they come through the door.

USE OF DATA ON VISITS

Figures on the number of people who visit the library each year can be a very powerful tool in demonstrating demand for your services. While librarians tend to think more often of circulation as a measure of usage, visits may be a more persuasive number to present to your mayor, city councillor, or county commissioner. While circulation and reference represent demand for information and resources, visits represent people. To those who authorize funding for libraries, each person who visits the library is a potential voter.

Beyond their use as a public relations tool, visitor statistics, especially when kept on a daily—or even hourly—basis, will also indicate when the public is most likely to come through the library doors. This can help effectively allocate staff so that more staff is present when the library is busiest and so that the library can be open as many hours as possible. For example, after analyzing your data on visits, you might find that Thursday evenings are very slow and Saturday mornings are very busy. This information might stimulate a decision to close Thursday evenings and open a full day on Saturday instead. Most often, the statistics will simply bear out staff observations. In such cases, the data can be valuable in defending or advocating management decisions to others who are not in the library every day, such as board members or the city manager.

PROGRAM ATTENDANCE AND ATTENDANCE AT JUVENILE PROGRAMS

Program attendance is the number of persons of all ages who attend programs in the library. Since 1993, juvenile program attendance has also been a separate FSCS data element. *Attendance at juvenile programs* is defined as the number of persons of all ages attending programs aimed at a juvenile audience. Note that this is not the same as the number of juveniles attending programs.

Program attendance is measured by simply counting the house at programming events. To ensure that this measure is accurate, be sure to designate a staff member to make a count of the house every time there is a program. So that the presenter can concentrate on the program, the counting should be done by someone other than the presenter whenever possible. Make sure that the counter understands that all persons attending the program (except library staff presenting the program) should be counted. To record peak number of persons attending, take the count a few minutes after the program begins, after most of the audience has arrived, but before they start to leave. If possible, record any persons arriving at the program after the count was taken.

Program attendance information is a key output statistic, especially in those libraries where programming has been identified as a high-priority service. Like visits, it represents persons using services as opposed to such statistics as circulation and reference, which represent resource uses. As pointed out above, elected officials who authorize funding for the library are often surprised by and certainly very interested in figures that demonstrate that a significant portion of their electorate is in the library.

INTERLIBRARY LOANS

Because they are FSCS data elements, your state will require that you report both the number of items which you provided to other libraries and the number provided to your patrons from other libraries. The definitions are the same for each of these categories. The materials are provided on request and include both library materials and copies of library materials (usually photocopies). To count an item as an interlibrary loan, the transaction must occur between two libraries that are not under the same administration. For this reason, a transaction between branches of the same system, for example, should not be reported as an interlibrary loan. Finally, it is not always necessary to count only items loaned as interlibrary loans. Photocopies—which should be counted as interlibrary loans when sent from one library to another—are provided without the expectation that they will be returned.

IN-HOUSE USE OF LIBRARY MATERIALS

If collected consistently and sensibly, data on the in-house use of materials can yield very useful information. Unfortunately, since this is not an FSCS data element, there is no nationally recognized standard for collecting the data. Furthermore, there is no consensus among library researchers that even supports the validity of this statistic, especially as an indicator of usage. This is due to several factors, including the difficulty of agreeing upon a method of collection, the questionable reliability of any method of collection, and complications caused by the proliferation of electronic-based resources in the library.

Nevertheless, many states require that these data be collected and reported. Further, many libraries collect these data for their own internal use. Many libraries, especially larger urban libraries with heavy walk-in traffic (as contrasted with suburban libraries to which patrons primarily drive), have found that circulation is only a partial indication of usage. These libraries have observed that significant use of their collection is by persons who never check out any items. These patrons may also be reluctant to approach staff members for help or simply not require assistance. These users may be regular customers who stop off daily to read the newspaper or browse the magazine rack.

They may be persons who stop in every several days to check on the performance of their investments in a financial reference source. They may be students or others who customarily use one or two reference resources for all of their work. Capturing only circulation of materials leaves out all of these perfectly legitimate uses of library resources. Increasingly, libraries have felt the need to capture this usage, not only as a way of demonstrating the importance of these materials and services, but also to track shifts in usage away from circulating materials.

The problem arises, however, in how best to measure this usage. The measure requires a count of the number of items used by patrons in the library. The most commonly encountered method is to count the number of items left out in the library. Since this is a very labor-intensive process (and staff is stretched thin already), libraries usually set aside either one or two representative weeks in the year to collect and count the number of items pulled from the shelves by patrons and left lying around the library. Usually states recommend April and October as sampling periods. Again, these may or may not be representative months in your library. You should pick months for sampling that you feel are the most representative of the average monthly usage.

Researchers and library statisticians are quick to point out that this collection method is flawed in several ways. First, just because an item was pulled from the shelf doesn't mean that the patron used it (though it could similarly be contended that all items checked out of the library are not necessarily read). Second, patrons often tend to ignore signs to the contrary and reshelve their own materials, especially magazines and newspapers. Finally, detractors argue that this method does not address in-house use of such electronic resources as CD-ROMs, which are coming to occupy an increasingly important role in libraries.

Nevertheless, when consistently collected and clearly defined, in-house use can, at the very least, contribute to a more well rounded picture of how your patrons use the collection. This, in turn, will lead you to important conclusions about how to build services, define long-range and strategic planning efforts, and market your services to the community. The data will also supplement circulation data as a public relations tool in showing library use. This may be particularly important for libraries with below-average circulation.

7 STAFF AND SALARY INFORMATION

Your state library annual report will ask a number of questions about staffing in your library. The number of staff, the number of librarians, the ratio of professional to nonprofessional staff, and salary information are all vital library statistics, especially for developing a picture of national or statewide trends.

STAFFING INFORMATION

FULL-TIME EQUIVALENTS (FTEs)

Your state probably asks you to report staffing information in terms of full-time equivalents, or FTEs. *Full-time equivalent staffing* simply means the total hours worked by staff in a normal week divided by the number of hours in a full-time week. For example, let's say your full-time workweek is 40 hours. You have 3 full-time staff and 3 part-time staff who work 20 hours each and a fourth part-timer, a page, who works 10 hours per week. You would have 4.75 FTEs. The calculation would look like this:

$$40 + 40 + 40 + 20 + 20 + 20 + 10 = \frac{190}{40} = 4.75$$

Because of the mixture in most libraries between full- and part-time staff, this is the most meaningful way to compare staffing. Reporting staffing in terms of full-time equivalents gives a much more accurate picture of the true extent of staffing than reporting the number of employees would.

Using FTEs presents one problem, especially when comparing data for different parts of the country. The problem arises because to calculate FTEs, libraries use their normal workweek. That number tends to vary between 35 and 40 hours per week depending on the library and, especially, on the part of the country. In many parts of the country—in the Northeast, for example—the commonly accepted workweek is nine to five, or 35 working hours per week. In other parts of the country—especially the South and the West—40 hours is considered a full workweek. And despite regional trends, employers are free to set their workweek at a different number of hours—37 1/2 hours per week being the third most common workweek.

This variability in the workweek tends to defeat the purpose of using FTEs. Unless you know what a given library considers a full-time workweek, what you call an FTE might really be less or more staff than what another library considers an FTE. Even with this variation, however, using FTEs is still a much more accurate way to record and compare staffing levels than number of employees where the differences in hours worked may be much greater than 5 hours per week.

In reporting the number of FTEs for the following categories, you will have to find out for what date your state requires that you report. Because you would not report all staff who worked at the library during the year if you had had a number of turnovers in staff, most states ask that you report staff for the last day of the fiscal year.

NUMBER OF LIBRARIANS

FSCS asks that states report the number of public library staff who hold master's degrees conferred by programs of library and information studies accredited by the American Library Association (ALA-MLS). This information has a number of uses. In the absence of any other relevant professional credential, the number of ALA-MLS librarians assesses the level of training available to library users. When coupled with salary information, we can monitor the progress of professional librarian earning power. We can draw regional comparisons of the use and compensation of persons holding a graduate degree in library science and thereby assess the ongoing occupational outlook for the profession both regionally and nationwide.

As with most matters involving education, income, and job competition, the emphasis placed on the MLS degree is somewhat controversial. Many communities do not staff their libraries with people who have MLSs. Either they are not required to do so by state law, or they choose not to do so because they cannot attract or cannot afford a professional librarian. Added to this is the fact that some library workers are offended by the emphasis on "professional librarians." In many cases, these individuals think that they are capable, competent, and paid for their work so that they deserve to be recognized as "professional" librarians.

Most state agencies recognize this reality. For this reason, states generally recognize as librarians those persons holding the title of librarian, whether or not they have ALA-MLSs. This is why FSCS asks not only for the number of staff members holding ALA-

MLSs, but also the number of staff who go by the title of librarian. Because FSCS asks for the information in this way, it is likely your state will ask you to report not only the number of FTEs with the ALA-MLS, but also the number of FTEs going by the title of librarian.

Your state may be one of many that requires ALA-MLS librarians in certain libraries. The most common scenario is that the state will impose a requirement that libraries above a population threshold—those serving 10,000 persons or more, for example—must have at least one staff member with an ALA-MLS. As in other areas of minimum criteria, failure to comply might jeopardize your library's accreditation or eligibility for state aid or carry some other negative consequence. If you are unsure whether your state has such a requirement, be sure to check with your state library before completing your annual report.

ALL OTHER PAID STAFF

Your state will also ask that you report the number of FTEs who are not librarians. This number will include not only those employees who perform library-related functions, but also plant operations staff, such as custodial and security staff. You should only report persons who are paid from the library's budget. In other words, do not count persons who work for the library but who are paid by some other entity, such as the city, county, or some other third party. As in all staff matters, you should report as of the date your state specifies, probably the last day of the fiscal year (the national standard). And remember to report FTEs, not number of persons working for the library.

VOLUNTEERS

Your state may ask that you report on volunteers working at the library. They may ask that you report the total number of volunteer hours worked during the year, or they may want the number of FTEs. Your state may want you to include with volunteer hours any hours paid for by an entity other than the library or the funding authority. Read your annual report instructions carefully to find out how you should report volunteer hours. Even if your state does not require you to report volunteer hours, you may collect them for your own information. For many libraries, volunteers are a major source of labor and require a commitment of staff time for training. For these reasons, many libraries document volunteer hours even when not required to do so by the state.

If your library is typical, your volunteers work occasional and erratic hours. Also, you may have a number of persons volunteering at your library, some who come week after week for years and others who come only once or twice or show up very rarely. For these reasons, you will probably have to develop a form to use in tracking volunteer hours. To make recording their hours easier, require volunteers to sign in and out each time they come to work. A sample form to use in collecting volunteer hours is included in Appendix A.

SALARY INFORMATION

While salary information is not required by the federal government, many states collect information on staff compensation. Most commonly this information is requested for the head librarian, but it is not uncommon for the annual report to request salary data for other staff members also, as well as information on the library's salary range for professional positions.

This is undoubtedly the most sensitive question on the annual report form. Understandably, many directors are very hesitant to report their salaries to the state, especially when they know the information will be published for all the world to see in the state library's annual statistical publication. On the other hand, when it comes to lobbying the city council or the county commissioners for more money, directors find it very helpful to be able to compare their salaries to those of other directors in neighboring towns or in similar towns across the state.

Remember that you always have the right to refuse to answer any question on the annual report form, and I don't know of any state that makes library accreditation or eligibility for state aid dependent on reporting the director's salary, but you should consider answering the question. It just might help a colleague get a raise in her salary. Chances are, your salary is public information anyway, so someone could find out if she really tried.

If your state asks you to report this information, it very likely also asks you to say how many hours per week you work. If a librarian makes $25,000 per year, it makes a big difference whether he works 20 or 40 hours per week. Keep this in mind when using salary data. If there are persons in your sample who work fewer hours than a full-time week, you should equalize the information according to the number of hours in *your* full-time week. The only exception to this would be if you do not work a full-time week, in which case you would equalize the salaries to whatever your workweek would be. In other words, if you work 30 hours per week, express the salaries of the other librarians reported as though they worked 30 hours per week (for example, show an annual salary of $30,000 as $22,500).

THE VALUE OF STAFFING AND SALARY INFORMATION

Data on library staffing and salary can have several very useful purposes. First, it is a library input measure. The level of staffing in a given library is part of the picture of service provided to library patrons. In fact, for most libraries, personnel is the single most costly item and as such is deserving of special attention. When comparing your library to another library, staffing measures can be very illustrative. You can use this information to calculate several figures that tell a great deal about the effectiveness of your library program, staff loads, and service provided to the public.

Library Staff per Capita

Because a simple calculation of staff per capita would yield a very small number, this is frequently calculated as FTEs per thousand of population. This measure can then be used to compare your library's staffing per capita with other similar libraries. This number is calculated by dividing the number of FTEs by the population served (FTEs/[population]). If calculated on each thousand of population, divide the number of FTEs by the population divided by 1,000 (FTEs/[population/1,000]).

For example, if your staff is 10 FTEs and your population served is 10,000, the FTEs per capita would be 0.001, and FTEs per thousand of population would be 1.

Population per Library Staff

While this statistic seems to be simply the inverse of staff per capita, it really has a different purpose altogether. Measuring population per staff yields information on staff load and is used to support the argument that staff members are overworked and patrons are inadequately served. The calculation is made by dividing the population served by the number of FTEs (population/ FTEs). In the above example of 10 FTEs and 10,000 population, this number would be 1,000.

Circulation per Staff

One of several measures of service per staff, this statistic demonstrates the relative effectiveness of the staff, the workload carried by the staff, and the need for additional staff. For specific programs, you could change this measure to program attendance per staff, reference transactions per staff, or any other service output per staff. The calculation is made by dividing the service measure by the number of FTEs (circulation/FTEs).

Comparative Salaries

This is a favorite of library directors at budget time. The most common method is to pick a population range that includes your library and compare library director salaries for that set of libraries. If you create a spreadsheet with this information, you can easily sort the data to find out where your library ranks by population served, then re-sort it to find out where your salary ranks. If you can tell your board that your library ranks 5th out of the sample group of 15 libraries, but your salary ranks 12th out of the same 15, then your board is likely to agree that you need a raise (see the discussion of ranking in Chapter 10). Two cautions: First, use a population range that puts your library's population served in the middle of the group; and second, be sure that your numbers are favorable to your argument before you distribute them.

This and previous chapters have discussed what is on your annual report form and how to collect and report it. Chances are we've covered most of the items requested by your state. If there are other items that are causing you collection problems, remember that you can always call your state library staff for information, guidance, and technical assistance. Keep the numbers of key state library consulting staff close to your phone and call them whenever you have problems. Refer to Appendix A for sample forms to use for collecting data for your annual report.

8 DECIDING WHAT ELSE TO COLLECT

With few exceptions—like hours of access—we have covered just about every type of data that your library will report to satisfy the national data collection effort. We have also discussed a number of items that might be collected by your state only. There are many other areas that we could have covered, areas that might be on your form. Some states collect extensive data about resource sharing, some ask questions about the status of your planning activities, some want more specific information on programs and services offered, and many have at least one or two questions about the size and age of your building.

To review, the following data items have been previously covered:

- administrative information (name, address, etc.)
- income
- local government income
- expenditures
- capital income and expenditures
- salary and benefits expenditures
- collection expenditures
- other expenditures
- collection
- circulation
- reference
- library visits
- interlibrary lending
- in-library use
- staffing

And, in several cases—such as income, collection size, and staffing—we have discussed several variations or subtotals within the element.

These categories of data collected from other libraries are available to you. In most cases, this information will be included in a statistical publication from the state library; in others, the data will not be published, and to get them you will have to ask for them directly from the state. You should never be too shy to ask for statistics from your state library. The data collected on your annual report form are, of course, public information. State library staffs tend to feel that a local library's participation in the annual survey earns them the right to ask for the information they need and to have it provided in a prompt and friendly manner. A big part of my job in Texas is running customized data charts from the Texas public library statistical data base whenever anyone calls. I place a high priority on answering requests for statistical data from local public libraries, and I think my colleagues in other state libraries do the same.

There will come a time, however, when you will face a frustrating obstacle. You will want data that you do not have—that nobody has. A hypothetical example of such a situation might unfold thus:

The mayor called the library director, Judy, with an urgent request that she report to the city council Tuesday night on how many library materials are checked out to borrowers who don't live in the city. He also wanted the same information compared to neighboring towns. Judy thought she collected those data for her annual report to the state, but upon reviewing the form, she found that she had not collected them. This meant that she either had to generate the data or face the mayor empty-handed. First, Judy checked her automated circulation system. She spent several hours reading the manual and talking to customer support before she figured out that she could not get the information because she had not coded her patron records. Meanwhile Judy called several of the surrounding towns and found that four of the six keep track of nonresident borrower circulation. Finally, Judy was reduced to sampling every user for the next four days to derive an estimate for nonresident circulation. As she went to the Tuesday night meeting, she hoped the mayor and council wouldn't ask too many hard questions about her data.

Obviously this scenario could have been different if Judy had been able to collect the data she needed to make the presentation, but we cannot possibly be prepared for every situation. And more important, it is not possible nor would it be wise to collect volumes of data just because you might need them some day. Chances are you already collect data you will never use. Still, you can see from the example—and you probably know from your own experience—there will be times when you will want to know something about your library that you cannot determine from the statistics you have been collecting and sending to the state library all these years. So how do you decide what other data you will need to collect? How do you decide what—among the range of data that you could collect—will be the most valuable for you?

The trick of knowing what data to collect depends on so many factors that there is no easy or right answer. Many of these factors relate to your local situation: the temperament of your library board, mayor, and other town officials; community interests and needs; and the roles you have chosen for your library.

While there are no easy answers, there are informed choices that you can make that can minimize the chance that the scenario above will happen to you. These choices begin with a thorough examination of your situation *before* you start collecting data. As in most other management matters, you should not try to do this all alone. Discuss it with your staff, the library board, and your colleagues in other towns. And, to protect yourself, it's a good idea to have the approval and support of your library board before engaging in any extensive data collection projects.

Let's look first at the questions you need to consider before collecting data, then turn to the types of data you could collect to meet your specifications.

QUESTIONS TO CONSIDER BEFORE COLLECTING NEW LIBRARY DATA

Do You Need the Figures to Support Planning?

Chapter 1 discussed the relation among library statistics, planning, and role-setting. Statistics are an indispensable tool in determining the library's roles in the community. Is this your situation? Are you trying to discover how the library is used by the community, why people come into the library, and what services and materials they expect to find when they come into the library? If this is the case, it is likely that your choices about the data you collect will focus on measurement and analysis of existing services. For example, it may not be enough to know that reference services are popular; you may need to know the precise subject areas in which patrons are asking for reference assistance.

Do You Need Statistics to Support Role-Setting?

You may be further along in your planning cycle. You may have already completed an evaluation of existing services and written a long-range or strategic plan for the library. In that plan you may have set out some roles for the library. These roles are meant to direct decisions about funding, staffing, and other aspects of library management. Now you must evaluate the extent to which those decisions support your chosen roles. You will need data to do this. In your planning process you should already have identified certain success indicators, but it is very possible that you now need other data. If this is your situation, the roles you have chosen for your library will drive your decisions about what data to collect. For example, if you have chosen children's services as a primary role for the library, it is unlikely that you will be very interested in collecting additional data on use patterns of adult reference materials.

What Is the Nature of Your Community?

As in so many areas of library management, it is vital to know and understand the nature of your community. Is it an aging community or comprised mainly of young families? Is it a commuter town or a factory town? Rural, suburban, or urban? What is the educational profile of the town? Do most residents live in apartments or single-family houses? This is just a sampling of the many demographic questions you might ask about your town. You could probably answer most of these questions off the top of your head, while others may take some thought, and some of the answers may surprise you. But thinking about the kind of community you serve will raise some important questions about use of your services. These are the questions that your mayor and city council are considering as well. These questions are also closely linked to planning and role-setting efforts. Knowing the nature of your community is vital to determining the services your library will offer.

Is Your Community Stable or in Transition?

If you community is stable (that is, changing little over the years), then the planning and role-setting you did three years ago may still be valid. If, however, your community is in transition, you will probably need different information about how patrons are using your library than you did a few years ago. Is the socioeconomic profile of your community changing? Do you serve an urban area where residents are moving out to the suburbs? Are you a suburban area facing an influx? Have building or zoning patterns changed? As the community you serve changes, you will need and want different information about your library and how it is used. These types of concerns may have motivated the mayor in our example above to ask Judy for information on nonresident use of the library.

What Are the Areas of Interest of Your Library Board?

Ideally, your library board represents a cross-section of the community. They bring to their duties certain interests and concerns. The interests of your library board may very well drive your decisions about what you want to know about your library program. There may be members of your library board who are interested in adult education, automation, or children's services. These areas of interest may affect the direction of library activities.

What Are the Political Trends in Your Community?

Even the smallest communities are affected by the winds of political change. Perhaps there is an anti-tax sentiment brewing that could threaten your new building plans. Or maybe there is a drive to consolidate city services that could result in the combining of the school and public libraries. What is happening in local politics will ultimately affect the public library. You must also be aware of the interests and concerns of local elected officials. For example, are there sensitive issues in the upcoming city council elections that could affect the library? It may be very important to judge ahead of time the direction of these trends and begin to gather needed data in the event that your program is challenged or otherwise affected.

What Are Your Patrons Saying?

You may actively solicit suggestions from your patrons, but even if you don't, chances are that you will hear from them anyway. Even the most offhand comments can indicate dissatisfaction with your library and can, ultimately, lead to decisions about what data to collect. If, for example, you hear someone complain that he cannot find books that are listed in the catalog, then perhaps an inventory is needed. If people complain that they can never find a free public access terminal, perhaps a study of terminal use would be helpful. Library data can support decisions that will bring the public better service, but you must first identify the problem areas where service needs improvement.

What Is Your Staff Saying?

Listen to your staff, especially if your library is big enough that you do not regularly meet the public. Your staff—especially those at the circulation desk and in other public service positions—is in a position to hear what your customers are saying about your services. So-called frontline staff members are sensitive to the public's complaints since they have to face those comments daily. Also take seriously your staff's observations about use patterns, times of peak business, staffing levels, the adequacy of the collection, and any other area in which they are directly involved.

If you're thinking that these questions sound like they belong to a planning project, then you are right on target. Data collection is inextricably tied to the library's planning and role-setting efforts. A planning effort, however, when done correctly, will be much more elaborate and involved than these questions imply. Still, for the purposes of deciding what data to collect, these questions will serve as a starting place to consider the nature of the library's community, the political environment, the attitudes and interests of key players, and the needs and wishes of the library's clientele.

WHAT ADDITIONAL DATA SHOULD BE COLLECTED?

Assuming that you have asked some of the questions above and you have some sense of what you need to know more about, then you need to decide what you will collect. There are basically two ways that you can expand your data collection effort. You can collect in entirely new areas or you can strive for greater detail about what you already collect. These are not mutually exclusive, and you will likely choose some combination of the two.

It may well be that you need data in some new area in which you have never previously collected. For example, if you install an on-line public access catalog, you may want to measure use of the catalog. You may want to know, for example, how many people use the catalog, how long it takes to do a typical search, or the success rate for searches. This would, of course, be new data for your library to collect, data that would be valuable in evaluating the success of a new service—namely, the on-line catalog.

But often, you will find that you already collect in the right areas; you just don't have enough detail. The example of Judy and the nonresident borrowers illustrates this situation. Like most librarians, she kept circulation records, but when the mayor called, she realized that she did not keep sufficiently detailed circulation records to provide easily the data he requested. To satisfy the mayor's request, Judy would have to have kept not only total circulation, but also circulation by patron type.

Let's take another example of the way you could find more detail in the data you already collect. Let's say you want to analyze work load at the reference desk so that you can staff it more effectively. It is not sufficient to know only the total annual number of reference questions, the number of questions per month, or even the number per week. What you will need to know is the number of questions asked each hour of the day. With this information, over a period of a few weeks, you will be able to see when the desk tends to be busiest and staff it accordingly. This can be done only by tallying reference transactions per hour; any less frequent tally would be useless. (See Appendix A for a sample form for recording hourly reference transactions.)

Of course, you will have many options when it comes to adding detail to your data collection effort. Rather than collecting greater detail about the frequency of reference statistics, you might choose instead to record the subject areas of each question. This information would be valuable in making collection development decisions. Rather than collecting circulation data by patron class (such as children, adults, or some other group of persons, as Judy will be doing from now on), you might prefer to know what classes of materials are being borrowed. This would answer a number of questions about use of the library's materials. In this way, you can analyze the circulation statistics in a different way. Remember, it is still circulation we are talking about. Whether your subtotals are for classes of patrons, or classes of materials, or both, they all add up to the same total annual circulation figure.

You can see that the possibilities are endless. Circulation, reference, program attendance, in-house library use, visits—just about any service measure can be refined into more specific data that can be collected by hour, or by class of patron, or by type of question, or by some other criteria. Input data can also be collected in greater detail. For example, rather than just recording the total number of items added to the collection, you can record the number of items by classification area.

It would be very difficult (not to mention pointless) to review every statistic that you might consider for collection, but there are several broad categories you should consider. What follows is a list of those categories, a few sample statistics to illustrate each, and a note on the potential use of those data.

Expenditures

Break out income and expenditure data to capture greater detail for budgeting and planning purposes. This is relatively simple to do with either manual or automated bookkeeping methods. Chances are you already have much greater detail in expenditure data than you need for your annual report to the state library. You should periodically reevaluate whether expense categories you use yield the information you really need.

- *Collection expenditures* can be subdivided by subject area, by classification (that is, 100s, 200s, 300s, and so on), or by type of materials purchased (books, serials, videos, etc.). This is particularly important data if you or your board want to track the effectiveness of increased funding in certain areas of the collection.
- *Other expenditures* can be tracked in specific areas, such as automation expenditures, utilities, furniture and equipment, and so forth. Again, chances are your bookkeeping system already captures these, but be sure they are the data you really need.

Collection

Estimate the number of items in each category of your collection by using one of the methods suggested in Chapter 5.

- *Collecting by format.* Collection data can be kept by item format. For example, determine the number of items in your books-on-tape collection. This is valuable as a way both to analyze the relative strengths of the collection and to target certain areas for expansion. Combined with corresponding circulation data, you can measure the impact of localized collection development on circulation of those items.
- *Age of collection.* If your automated system cannot give you this data, it can be determined by sampling. This statistic can be very valuable for collection development purposes, but only if you can make very localized measurements of the age of the collection. A five-year-old book in the social sciences may be too old to retain, while a five-year-old biography may not be.

Service outputs

It is most likely that if you are considering collecting new statistics about your library, they will be output measures. These are just a few of the areas in which you could collect data:

- *In-library use.* Usually measured by sampling items left out in the library on two or more typical weeks per year. Once an FSCS data element, this statistic is still collected in a number of states and can be valuable for measuring total usage of the collection, especially in libraries with significant walk-in traffic.
- *Use of automated services.* There are many ways to measure this, and most can be logged automatically. Consult

your automation vendor to see if he can install a program in your OPAC to measure the number of sessions (usually done by logging certain keystrokes, such as use of the Reset key). Your Internet vendor or in-house support staff can tell you what measures you can capture by automated means. These will probably include number of Telnet accesses, number of files accessed or transferred, and the number of hours on-line. If Internet usage in your library is mediated, staff can keep a separate tally of requests filled using that medium as well as the number of electronic files transferred or other specific uses, though this is much less preferable to automated counts. Callers dialing into the library can also be logged.

- *Circulation.* The value of keeping circulation figures according to patron class (such as circulation to juveniles, nonresidents, etc.) and materials class (such as fiction, nonfiction, picture books, or by Dewey area) has already been discussed.

- *Reference.* Again, this can be tallied by time of day, type of request, or library department. You can also measure the average length of time taken to answer each reference question, or the reference completion rate, which is defined in *Output Measures for Public Libraries* (p. 94) as "the proportion of reference questions successfully completed." All these measures and more can be captured by the use of a reference form to record each reference question received. Such a form can track a tremendous amount of information about the reference process. See Appendix A for an example of such a form.

- *Registered borrowers.* Once, when I was a library director, I attended a city council discussion of a new library building. During the meeting, the mayor abruptly singled me out of the audience to ask me how many residents were registered to borrow books. I guessed and, luckily, was not far off. After that, I kept careful tabs on the number of registered borrowers. If your state does not ask you to keep track of the number of registered borrowers, you should consider this measure for your own internal use. The percentage of the population of your service area that are registered library borrowers can be one indication of the library's relevance to the community. For this statistic to be valid, patron records must be current within three or fewer years, depending on the degree of transience in the community. To be meaningful, this measure is usually expressed as a percentage of the population—for example, "45% of the population of our community are registered borrowers."

- *Fill rates.* Fill rates refer to the percentage of times a patron request or need is satisfied. Fill rates can be measured in a number of ways, including author and title fills, browser fills, or subject fills. Fill rates are measured by asking patrons whether they found what they were looking for. In some limited situations, fill rates can be measured by automated means by capturing searches on a library's OPAC, but most frequently, they are measured by conducting interviews of patrons to determine if they found what they were looking for in the library. Fill rates can be measured for the collection as a whole or for discrete parts of the collection. The rate of fills is a service output that can indicate responsiveness of the collection to the public's needs. *Output Measures for Public Libraries* recommends the use of three specific fill rates: title, subject, and browser fill rates.

ABOUT SURVEYS

Most of the statistics we have discussed so far are collected by staff in the course of their daily routine. Other data, such as fill rates, cannot be collected effectively without a survey. Surveys, while they can certainly yield valuable data about customer satisfaction, are a different kind of statistic for a number of reasons. First, surveys—especially interviews—cannot practically be conducted by staff members in the course of discharging their normal duties. Second, survey questions tend to change, so it is very hard to track survey data historically, which (as we will discuss in Chapter 10) is an important aspect of data analysis. Third, with the exception of fill rates, surveys do not generally yield quantifiable data about the library that are as concrete as, say, the number of items checked out. Finally, survey validity is subject to a number of pitfalls that result from the subjectivity of respondents, the types of questions asked, and the way responses are recorded.

All the same, surveys can provide information that is not available by any other means, but because they do not measure objectively defined and captured data, they must be considered as qualitatively different from library statistical data and, as such, outside the scope of this book.

A FINAL WORD ABOUT JUDY AND HER AUTOMATED SYSTEM

One final point remains to be made about the case of Judy, the librarian from our example who had not collected the data the mayor wanted on nonresident borrowers. Even though Judy had not collected that data, she could have made choices that would have made the job of reconstructing the data much easier. Most commercial library automation systems allow patron records to be coded by type of borrower. Even if they are never used, purchasing the option from the vendor can make it far easier to generate reports that break down the data according to these criteria.

The moral of Judy's story is to be prepared for the chance that someday you might want to capture data that you do not currently need. When you create the specifications for your automated systems, build in more options than you think you will ever need. Once you buy the system, you will likely find it costly and cumbersome to have these options added; if you tell the vendor ahead of time, however, they can probably be easily included in your system. If you can't decide what you will need and you do not have an independent consultant helping you select a system, call some other librarians in your state or region and ask about their systems and the report-writing features they included in the specifications for their system.

EXTERNAL DATA SOURCES

The time may come when you will want data that you cannot collect. You may want to compare your library to other libraries around the state, to locate economic or demographic data about your community or your area, or to find any of a number of other types of data. These data will help you analyze your services, understand your community, conduct strategic and long-range planning, and perform cost and market analyses. There are several sources for such data.

The State Library

While your state library probably publishes a book of library statistics, there will be a number of times when you should consider calling for more information. Typically, the state library requests some information from libraries that is never published. Also, there will be a lag between when the data is collected and its publication. It may well be that the state library has more recent data available in electronic format than what has been printed. Also, state library staff may be able to pull the data for you and send it to you in either an electronic file or in a printout. Finally, the state library tracks data from a number of other sources that might be of help to you. It is always worthwhile to see what they have available or to get their recommendation for other places to hunt for the needed information.

Census Data

Most librarians are aware that the U.S. Census Bureau's decennial census is a treasure trove of statistics. Information down to the smallest local unit is available on dozens of demographic variables in such broad categories as income, education, ethnicity, household composition, and age. Your nearest U.S. documents depository will carry a series of CD-ROMs of these data that can be easily selected, downloaded to diskette, and incorporated into your spreadsheets. Increasingly, these files are available on the Internet as well.

State Data Center

The only problem with the census is that it is done only once every ten years. This situation causes the value of the data to decrease each year of the decade. This is where the state data center comes in handy. Each state has a data center. Find the location of the data center for your state and keep the phone number handy. The state data center performs ongoing updates and compiles supplementary figures to the U.S. Census, including an estimate of population for each locality in the state beginning around the fourth year of the decade and then updating it every other year after that. Once completed, the state data center estimates become official U.S. Census estimates of population. These should be available to you either from the state data center, the U.S. Census Bureau, or through a federal documents depository library in your state.

Other State and Federal Agencies

Many other state and federal agencies collect and report information that is of tremendous value to libraries. Most notably at the federal level, the Department of Commerce collects data on economic growth, wages and salaries, community profiles, price indexes, and much more information of potential value to libraries. In addition to the public library data it makes available, the U.S. Department of Education collects and publishes huge amounts of data regarding education. Because libraries are so closely related to the education process, these statistics are valuable. State departments of commerce and education will have similar types of data at the state level. Also, don't overlook whatever agency in your state collects information on local property values and taxation. These data can provide extremely interesting information about the local economy as well as local financial strength. Much of this information is available on the Internet as well as in the traditional print resources.

Chambers of Commerce

Frequently the local or regional chamber of commerce in your area will be the clearinghouse for a tremendous amount of local economic and demographic data. Similarly, each state has a chamber of commerce that monitors these figures on a statewide basis.

Library Research

As you go out searching for data, don't forget to check and see what is available within the library profession. Researchers working in library schools, in professional associations such as ALA and PLA, in federal agencies, and in state library agencies, produce a sizable body of data that is available to you. These data are published in library journals and in monographs from commercial and professional association presses. This research can be easily located through *Library Literature*, a periodical index available in print, on-line, and CD-ROM formats from the H.W. Wilson Company. Two standard sources of 2information are the U.S. Department of Education's *Public Libraries in the United States* and the Public Library Association's annual *Statistical Report*. Both are listed in the Bibliography.

"OKAY, SO WHAT DATA DO I WANT?"

In order to decide what data you need, you have to decide what situation you want more information about. And since—as I have said—data collection is a big commitment, especially for staffs already pushed to the limit, you must choose carefully. The chart below suggests the type of data you need to answer various questions about your library. It is not an exhaustive list by any means, but it will help you begin to think about how to match your data-collection effort to your information needs. For dozens of other data that could be collected, consult other works listed in the Bibliography of this book, especially *The Public Library Effectiveness Study* by Nancy Van House and Thomas Childers.

If you want to know about this . . .	Collect these data . . .
Patterns of library access	Library visits per capita Visits by hour Visits by outlet Type of use by hour Remote access (by patrons to the library via dial-up, Internet, etc.) Telephone information requests
Collection strength (general collection)	Items owned per capita Items owned by type or format Circulation per capita Interlibrary loan transactions Number of periodical titles Circulation by Dewey area Circulation by material type Circulation by format Title fill rate Browsers fill rate Subject fill rate Number of new materials added Age of collection Average time to fill reserves
Collection strength (reference)	Reference contacts Reader's advisor contacts Reference completion rate Referral rates Subject fill rate
Volume of use	Visits per capita Circulation per capita Number of circulations per visit Reference transactions per capita In-house use per capita Collection turnover rate (circulation/collection) Program attendance per capita Telephone information requests
Patterns of use	Visits by hour Program attendance by age Circulation by material type Interlibrary loan transactions Reference contacts by hour Contacts per public service desk In-library use by type of material In-library use by part of library

Adequacy of staffing
  (most measures meaningful only
  in comparison with other libraries
  of similar size)
	FTEs per thousand of population
	MLSs per thousand of population
	MLSs as percentage of total staff
	Circulations per FTE
	Reference requests per FTE
	Staff-to-use ratios per desk by hour
	Visits per FTE

Efficiency of staff	Reference turnaround time Interlibrary loan turnaround time Work load per staff (such as patrons assisted, circulations, items shelved, materials processed, etc.)

Children's services
  (dependent on roles chosen;
  see Virginia Walter, *Output
  Measures for Public Library
  Service to Children*)
	Children's program attendance per child
	Turnover rate of children's materials
	Children's library visits per child
	Building use by children
	Children's reference/information transactions per child
	Homework fill rate
	Class visit rate
	In-library use of children's materials per child

Adequacy of support	Income per capita Expenditures per capita Income by source Income relative to tax base Unit cost of services (ratio of expenditures to number of transactions) Materials expenditures per capita Personnel expenditures per capita Comparative salary data Turnaround times Materials availability Fill rates
Adequacy of facilities	Square footage per capita Visits per capita Hours of access Program attendance per capita Floor counts of users Adequacy of parking (lot counts; ratios of spaces to patrons, visits, etc.) Counts/surveys of persons with disabilities
Electronic access (volume and adequacy)	Number of on-line sessions Number of files accessed Number of electronic document transactions Number of uses of locally mounted data bases Number of remote log-ins to library services Availability of on-line catalogs Response times

Responsiveness to community needs	Demographics of community
	User demographics
	Program attendance per capita
	Visits per capita
	Circulation per capita
	Reference transactions per capita
	In-library use per capita
	Frequency of visits
	Visits per family
	Use of special services
	Use by outlet
	Percent of population registered

9 PUTTING YOUR DATA TO WORK

Now comes the fun part.

You've done the hardest work: you've gathered the numbers, trained the staff, made the hard choices about what new data to collect, filed your report with the state library. Now it's time to take a deep breath, relax, and have some fun playing with the fruits of your labor.

How do you do that? By letting your data tell a story about your library, the story you want it to tell. Perhaps you want to show that your staff is overworked, that you are underfunded, that you have long since outgrown your current facility, that your library is the most productive in the area, that the popularity of your story hours is at an all-time high, that nonresidents are not paying their fair share for library services. The possibilities are nearly endless. And regardless of what argument you are making about your library, if the data support your position, you will find statistics to be powerful and eloquent allies.

Before you use statistics to make your case, however, you have to decide exactly what you are trying to say, whom you are trying to convince, how much you know about your data, and whether you are using your numbers in the most effective way.

What Argument Do You Want to Make?

This is the most important question and worth careful consideration. When statistics are used effectively, they make a statement eloquently and directly, but careless use of the wrong data is distracting and will undermine rather than support your argument. Finding just the right data to support your point takes a lot of thought and trial and error. Later in this chapter we will explore some of the tried and true uses of data, but eventually you will want to find your own unique uses of statistics. Finding just the right numerical presentation to make your argument is very rewarding and worth some effort, but you have to be willing to discard a lot of failed efforts along the way.

What Process Would You Like the Data to Support?

The key word here is "process," not argument (we'll get to that in a moment). Chapters 1 and 8 discuss the various activities that could be supported with statistical information, including resource allocation, benchmarking, public relations, demonstration of need, evaluation, analysis of use patterns, and staff development. We will explore those more extensively later in this chapter, but the context in which you intend to use data will determine what data to select and how to present them.

Who Is Your Audience?

It makes a big difference whether the presentation you are preparing is for your library board, city council, the press, or the public. While you might use your data to brag to the public in your annual report about the popularity of your young adult programming series, you might present the same data slightly differently to the library board to justify a reallocation of funds from other programs into young adult services, then use the same data yet again to argue to the city council that your meeting room is too small to accommodate the demand for your programming.

How Good Are Your Data?

This is an important question in any context, but the answer may be critical depending on your audience. If you are arguing to an unsympathetic city or county government to increase your funding, you might expect hard questions about the reliability and source of your data. On the other hand, patrons are unlikely to question closely the source of data used to create a pie chart in your annual report brochure. But whatever your audience, it is important that you understand the reliability, timeliness, and accuracy of your data. Usually what you know about your data is linked to the source of the data. If you or your staff collected them, you have a general idea of how reliable they are. On the other hand, if you are using data collected by another library or agency for comparison purposes, you may not know so much about their reliability.

Now let's consider some of these issues in greater depth using examples.

MATCHING DATA TO PROCESS

What does this mean? It means that what you intend to use the data for will determine what data you select. Specific uses include resource allocation, demonstration of need, public relations, and benchmarking.

RESOURCE ALLOCATION

Resource allocation is a fancy management term that basically means deciding how to spend your money. Because we know that we do not have unlimited resources to do everything we would like to do, we have to make choices about how we will spend what we have. Effective library managers base those decisions on something other than personal likes and dislikes. Data on the use of our collections and services can provide an objective and demonstrable basis for making allocation decisions.

In larger libraries, these decisions may be handled by department managers who will have to decide which of their activities require more funding and which should be cut. The head of children's services, for example, will have to decide whether it is more effective to buy picture books or easy readers, whether to concentrate on preschool programming or craft times for older children, what format of audiovisual material is most popular, and whether a second computer for public use is justified.

The reference librarian will have to decide whether to purchase print or CD-ROM materials, which areas of the collection need attention, and how to staff the reference desk to provide adequate coverage at peak times.

Analyzing use patterns simplifies these decisions. In deciding how to allocate resources, the head of children's services will want to look at statistical measures such as the following:

- number of persons attending each program
- number of circulations broken down by Dewey area
- juvenile reference questions by subject area
- average age of collection by Dewey area

Meanwhile the head of reference will be looking at a similar set of criteria, including the following:

- number of reference questions by time of day
- number of reference questions by subject area
- fill rate for reference questions by subject area
- reference questions logged by time of day

This last item will influence decisions on how to staff the reference desk. The following table is an example of how information on the number of questions asked by time of day can be pulled together into aggregate data. Figure 9-1 shows the total number of reference transactions answered during each hour of the week for an entire year for a hypothetical small public library. The shaded areas indicate hours the library is closed.

Figure 9–1			Number of Reference Transactions per Hour				
	M	**T**	**W**	**Th**	**F**	**S**	**Total**
10:00	41	37	26	21	38	175	338
11:00	66	71	62	47	49	282	577
12:00	83	87	91	73	66	327	727
1:00	72	59	80	76	82	344	713
2:00	87	83	91	84	87	320	752
3:00	105	111	127	101	99	371	914
4:00	121	137	121	140	112		631
5:00	92	106	94	118			410
6:00	128		141				269
7:00	177		181				358
8:00	164		210				374
Total	1,136	691	1,224	660	533	1,819	6,063

Figure 9-1 could support two important resource allocation decisions. First, of course, it shows the hours that the desk is busiest, so it will help the director or head reference librarian determine when staff are most needed at the desk. For example, it would seem to be a good idea to make sure the desk is adequately staffed on Saturdays, when reference business skyrockets. Second, this tabulation shows an interesting pattern of reference use. Demand for reference services is greatest on Saturdays and weekdays after 3:00 p.m.—times when school is out. This would suggest that school students are heavy users of reference services (a statistical observation that is probably no surprise to the reference staff). Therefore, the second resource allocation decision supported by these numbers is the purchase of reference materials designed to support student needs.

Similarly, the director and staff will want to look at the following measures in deciding how to allocate resources.

- number of persons attending programs by type of program
- the unit cost of service outputs by program
- use patterns over time
- circulations (or other usage) per FTE staff compared to other libraries of similar size

- fill rates
- registered borrowers as a percentage of total residents

Any one of these or a dozen other measures can provide the library director with the information she needs to make decisions about how to spend limited funds. The library director will present these data only to the library board and usually then only as supporting documentation. Therefore, this use of data need not have high presentation quality. Simple tables and narrative descriptions are usually sufficient. In most cases it is not necessary to present the data in charts. Figure 9-2 would support the decision to purchase fewer reference materials in print and redirect these funds to purchasing information in electronic formats. A simple glance at the chart shows that more questions were answered using CD-ROM and Internet tools than by using all books and printed periodicals combined.

Figure 9–2 Sources Used to Satisfy Reference Requests						
Books	Periodicals print format	CD-ROM	Internet	Mixed formats	Referral	Total
1,045	1,394	2,204	634	509	187	5,973

DEMONSTRATION OF NEED

Demonstration of need might seem to be the same thing as resource allocation, but it is somewhat different. Resource allocation is a management decision that involves determining how to spend the money you have. Demonstration of need is an attempt to get more funding for your library or library department. This is frequently done by showing your usage compared to usage in other libraries or other library departments.

Managers of departments in larger libraries might have to demonstrate to their director the popularity of their services in relation to other departments of the library. For example, the coordinator of youth services might find the following measures useful in arguing for increased funding for the children's program.

- attendance at juvenile programs
- circulation of juvenile materials as a percentage of total circulation
- effect of programming on materials use
- correlation of spending on children's services to use of those services
- relative proportion of spending and use between children's services and the total library program

This last point is demonstrated in Figure 9-3.

Figure 9–3 Table Showing Demonstration of Need				
	Total Expenditures	Materials Expenditures	Circulation	Program Attendance
Children's and YA	$29,378	$7,000	36,332	1,266
% of Total	19%	27%	44%	91%

In this example, children's services account for a high percentage of total circulation and program attendance but a relatively low percentage of materials and total expenditures. The head of children's services could use these numbers to argue that a modest increase in the children's program could reasonably be expected to yield a higher return in usage than money spent elsewhere in the library.

Other departments will use data in other ways. The reference department will use other figures, such as:

- number of reference transactions
- number of materials used in-house
- number of uses of electronic resources
- number of reader's advisory consultations

Technical services, because they do not deal directly with the public, will have to use other measures of their work load. Technical services might use the following measures to indicate their effectiveness:

- number of new books processed
- number of books mended
- number of cards pulled from the catalog
- number of bibliographic records added to the catalog

Some of these measures will be meaningful only when viewed in a multiyear progression. If you can demonstrate that work load has been increasing steadily with no increase in staff, you can then argue more effectively for increased staff.

Branch managers will use the full range of these data and attempt to compare themselves to other branches in much the same way that autonomous public libraries tend to compare themselves to one another.

A library director will make similar arguments for the whole library, usually to the city council or city manager, by comparing the library to other city or county departments. Because you want to impress the target audience and because of the stakes involved, the presentation quality is important. Create tables that are simple and straightforward and that do not require a great deal of pondering to get the point. Charts should be attractive, simple, and easy to read and understand at a glance (which may be all they get from your city council).

Figure 9-4 is an example of using a statistical analysis to demonstrate need.

Figure 9–4 Using Statistics to Demonstrate Need				
	1991	**1992**	**1993**	**1994**
Circulation per capita	6.70	7.02	7.66	8.34
% Increase		4.8%	9.1%	8.9%
Expenditures per capita	$12.34	$12.86	$13.12	$13.15
% Increase		4.2%	2.0%	0.2%

Note that, like the table on children's services in Figure 9-3 above, Figure 9-4 presents an "up side" and a "down side." In this case, the up side is the increase in circulation; the downside is the flat funding of the library program. The director could use these circulation figures as a demonstration of the community's need for library services and thus argue that the city should meet that need with an increase in funding. Like the head of children's services in a previous example, the director of this library could argue that a minimal increase in funding could produce greater usage than increased funding of other city or county departments.

In demonstrating need, it is very important to show where possible that programs are popular but underfunded. Your message is a simple one: Demand for service is outstripping the library's ability to meet that demand. You thus must usually couple a demonstration of usage and demand with comparative figures from other libraries or library departments showing that you are lagging behind. Politicians like to support popular programs, and they like to fund projects that produce results in the way of usage.

PUBLIC RELATIONS

A common use of library data is in public relations efforts. This can take a variety of formats: annual reports, newsletters, newspaper articles, brochures, and fund-raising campaigns. Whatever the specific format, uses of data for public relations purposes will almost always be upbeat and positive and attempt to present the library as an active and popular service, where modest investments in tax dollars yield high usage figures. Figures that show the library program lacking in specific areas should be used sparingly in your publicity. Overall, your message should be, "Look at the good work we've done this year."

Nothing makes this case better than excellent service data. The following measures are frequently used to demonstrate the library's vitality and effectiveness:

- number of library materials checked out
- number of persons attending programs
- number of juvenile materials circulated
- number of reference questions answered
- number of children enrolled in the summer reading club
- number of persons visiting the library
- percentage of residents who are registered users
- unit costs per output
- number of persons receiving literacy instruction in the library

When using your data to prepare a brochure or newsletter, you will frequently find it helpful to use data from other sources. Sometimes you will want to compare your performance with that of other libraries. Other times you may wish to show your library as the most cost efficient of several city agencies. Another popular approach is to show the per capita amount spent for library service in your community as compared to other more common and perhaps trivial expenses. Figure 9-5 is an example of this type of presentation created by the Boulder (Colorado) Public Library and reproduced from their newsletter.

The exception to the advice above about being uniformly upbeat in public relations efforts is when the data are used for fundraising. The recurring message of a fund-raising campaign should be, "We are doing great things at the library, but with expanded resources (new building, etc.) we can do more." Those numbers you pulled together to demonstrate need to your city council will come in handy in creating materials for your fund-raising drive, but they must be used carefully and balanced with a positive message about what the library has accomplished.

Figure 9-6 was created by the Friends of Tennessee Libraries. This is the front and back of a bookmark produced as part of a lobbying effort. Again, in this approach we see the combination of positive and negative elements. One side of the bookmark lists

---

Figure 9–5 Page from the Boulder (Colorado) Public Library Newsletter

Are You Getting Your Money's Worth?

The .38 cent sales tax increase will cost the average Boulder citizen approximately **$17.00 per year**.

For **$17.00** you can buy:

1/3 of a filled pothole

OR

3/4 of a new hardback book (based on 1987 average cost)

OR

3/4 of a ticket to the CU Nebraska Football game

OR

1 tankful of gasoline

OR

1 extra large pizza with the works

OR

1 meal at a fast food restaurant for a family of 4

OR

2 1/4 months of the Daily Camera

OR

3 movie tickets with popcorn and soft drink

OR

3 parking tickets

OR

3 city aerobic classes & 3 1/2 lap swims

OR

Unlimited use of an improved and expanded Public Library, open full time, including free attendance at Library concerts and films.

EVERYBODY WINS

the many important services provided by Tennessee libraries, while the reverse describes how they lag behind libraries in the rest of the country. Tennessee lawmakers received this bookmark on Tennessee Library Association Legislative Day—along with a slice of homemade pie! While this publicity piece was designed for a state-wide situation, it can easily be adapted for local situations.

Data used for public relations purposes usually need to be very succinct and direct. The goal should be to convey a simple, straightforward message that can be easily understood at a glance.

Figure 9–6 Bookmark Created by the Friends of Tennessee Libraries

To serve the people of Tennessee here's what the PUBLIC LIBRARY provides with its piece of the pie:

* Access to technology
* Genealogical records
* Children's story hours
* Cost-free "how-tos"
* Summer reading programs
* Career information
* Information about legislative issues
* Travel guides
* Information about colleges
* Cookbooks
* Literacy tutoring
* Computers and software
* Investment information
* Special materials for the blind
* Legal information
* Reference books
* All kinds of maps
* Current newspapers/magazines
* Back newspapers/magazines
* Small business information
* Tapes and CDs
* Videotapes
* A quiet place to read

* and MORE

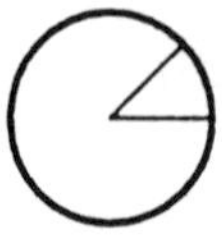

Here's how Tennessee stacks up with the rest of the country:

47th

in per capita funding for PUBLIC LIBRARIES

Tn. average: $7.44 per capita

Nat'l average: $17.83 per capita

From the state budget libraries get <u>less than</u> 1/10 of 1%

We deserve a **BIGGER** piece of the pie

FRIENDS OF TENNESSEE LIBRARIES

To do this, you should concentrate on one or two concepts that you are trying to convey. For example, compare the two charts in Figures 9-7 and 9-8. Figure 9-7 demonstrates the growth of programming for children, young adults, and adults over a five-year period.

This chart is confusing.

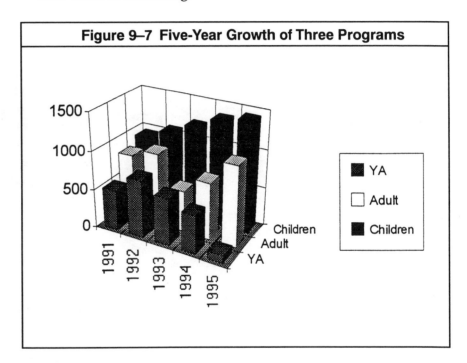

Figure 9–7 Five-Year Growth of Three Programs

There are so many different data points that no clear message is communicated. The reader must linger much too long and must work too hard to derive meaning from this display. There are too many distractions, such as the superfluous labels, the too-big legend box, the grids, and the unnecessary third dimension. Compare this chart to Figure 9-8 showing only the growth of children's programming. It clearly shows the obvious growth in popularity of children's programming.

Your presentations and public relations efforts should look as professional as possible. Most of the tables and charts in this book were created in Microsoft Excel. If you have access to a laser printer and software that can create graphs like the ones above, so much the better. If you do not, don't be discouraged. You can produce quality presentations using less expensive software, or you can probably find a Friend of the Library, trustee, or other interested community member who will help you run some charts on her computer. If all else fails, or if you want to have a particularly important presentation, you might consider contracting with

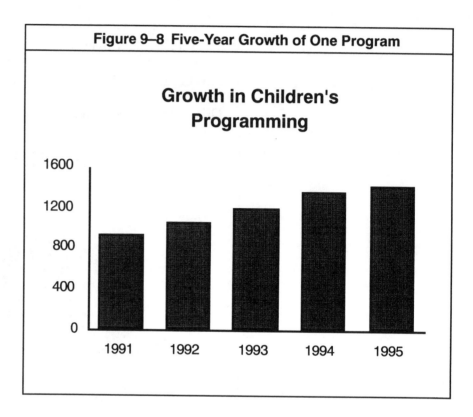

Figure 9–8 Five-Year Growth of One Program

a graphic artist to produce the materials according to your specifications.

Statistics can be effectively and attractively used in such public relations materials as annual reports, brochures, and newsletters. If this is what you have in mind, most likely you will want to display the information in attractive charts and graphs. Chapter 11 will discuss graphic displays of statistics.

BENCHMARKING

With the popularity of the management philosophy known as Total Quality Management (TQM), benchmarking has become a fashionable buzzword. Actually, the technique of benchmarking, under different names, has been around for quite a while. *Benchmarking* refers to the practice of measuring a particular activity in one organization, such as a library, and comparing the result with comparable measurements from other organizations or libraries. At intervals afterward, follow-up measures are checked against the benchmark libraries to determine the degree of improvement of the performance of the activity. The goal of the benchmarking process is to find ways to improve services and maximize resources and staff efficiency.

The core of benchmarking is a data collection effort that can be quite elaborate. This is partly because once a process has been identified for analysis, it should be broken down into *metrics*, or discrete tasks involved in the process. For example, a library may choose to apply a benchmarking test on the length of time it takes to get new books processed and into the circulating collection. This process involves a lot of smaller steps: unpacking the materials, putting wrappers on book jackets, cataloging, and so forth. Each of these steps involves different staff, but all that matters to the customer is how long it takes to get that new book they read about.

The steps involved in setting a benchmark include identifying a problem area to study and improve, finding a library or libraries to benchmark against, working with the staff of the benchmark library to study and measure their process, setting targets, measuring your library's productivity against the benchmark measures, and analyzing the results. It is easy to see that such a process requires a great deal of staff resources of the type generally only available in larger libraries.

Benchmarking is a statistical application that, when used as part of customer-driven focus, is a time-honored and reliable management strategy. In a larger organization, benchmarking will be an integral part of the team approach to improving demonstrably library service through measurement of a few key processes.

Benchmarking uses both inputs and outputs. Because inputs can be controlled, what can be learned from them is limited. On the other hand, outputs measure the success of a given decision in terms of service to the public. This makes sense in the context of an approach sensitive to customer service, such as TQM. Benchmarking measures can be as simple as the number of circulations or the number of persons attending programs, or they can be much more complicated and specific measures. What's important is that in selecting your benchmarks you identify the measure that is most indicative of the activity you are evaluating. For example, if you are trying to prove that your summer reading club is causing an increase in library visits by children, measure only visits by children and not all library visits.

The length of time covered by your benchmarking may vary greatly and will affect your choice of measures. Gradual changes should be expected to show gradual effects and thus must be measured over a much longer period of time. In longer periods of measurement, however, it is harder to clearly link cause and effect, especially if the measures are global, such as total circulation. The period covered by the benchmarking will also affect the measures you choose to monitor. If you are sampling a measure only occasionally over a short period of time, you can afford to use a more elaborate or highly specific measure that is time-consuming to collect. On the other hand, if the length of the benchmarking experiment is long or of indefinite duration, you will likely want to choose measures that are easier to collect or that you already have to collect for your state report.

Benchmarking is used almost exclusively as an internal management tool. Usually this information will be used only by managers within the library and sometimes by the library board. For this reason, it is usually not necessary for benchmark data to be presented graphically or with any kind of attention to publication quality. These are working numbers that will provide the basis of further decisions about resource management, planning, and goal setting. On the other hand, it very well could occur that your benchmarking efforts will yield data that can have a secondary application in a public relations presentation.

WHO IS YOUR AUDIENCE?

Making decisions on how to use your data will inevitably incorporate the answer(s) to this question. If you are studying your statistics to reach decisions about how to use your funds or to justify spending in a certain area, it is likely that your figures will be for use mainly by library staff and your board and for the occasional use of the city manager, mayor, council, county commissioners, or other city and county officials. Very rarely will reports produced for these purposes be published or otherwise shared with the public. The same holds true for data used in benchmark studies. These data are of use almost entirely by library staff.

If your presentation is part of a demonstration of need, it is likely that your audience will be your director if you are a department head or, if you are the director, officials of your funding authority, including the city manager, the county judge, the mayor and council, or even, in some cases, the state library. While these figures may not be widely published, it is likely that you will want to give more careful thought to presentation and approach than if you were using the data only for internal, managerial purposes.

Finally, in public relations uses, your audience will be the general public, probably through some sort of publication. While the audience for fund-raising campaigns will not always be the general public—sometimes it will be corporate donors, foundations, or other similar corporate entities—the effect on the way you present your data will be similar.

The audience you choose will shape the way you study, organize, present, and emphasize your data. You may begin to analyze data on your library without knowing your audience, but when it is time to share what you've learned about your library from your statistics, you will have to know to whom you will present your findings.

If your intended audience is other staff members, or you are collecting and analyzing data for your own use, you can handle the data in almost any format and any degree of complexity. Also, for internal purposes you don't need to put a "spin" on the data—that is, to make it tell a certain story. You and your staff want to know the up and down side of what you have learned about your library and its programs.

When you take data to the library board, you should sift through the complexity to pull out a few key elements. You may want to present these in either a tabular or graphic format. For the board, you want the data to be streamlined, and you want them to provide the informational basis for making decisions about the library.

When you take statistics to the mayor (or council, or city manager), you want the data to show the library in a favorable light, but also to identify those areas where the library risks falling behind without continued or increased financial support. You will want to present a few key facts pulled from your data. Your presentation should paint a clear and immediate picture of some aspect of the library. So long as it is clearly presented, the data can still be somewhat complex. For instance, you can show the relationship between two data series, such as income per capita and circulation per capita. The presentation you choose, whether tabular or graphic, will depend on the circumstances and what best suits the data being used.

When you use data in library publications, you will want to rely on just a few key facts about the library. Your aim is not to present complex research findings, such as complicated and multivariate data analysis, but a single chart or simple table that can be read and understood in an instant. In our world of "sound bites," the public has little time or inclination to mull over columns of numbers. They want to "cut to the chase" and "get to the bottom line." The data you prepare for your annual report or newsletter should be designed to provide key information at a glance. You will want to pick and choose among your data to show the library in its most favorable light.

HOW GOOD ARE YOUR DATA?

As we discussed briefly in the last chapter, when you begin to use your data to draw conclusions and make your arguments, it will become important for you to know the quality of your data. Why? Because sooner or later, someone will question the validity of your statistics.

Imagine that you are in the middle of an important presentation in front of the mayor and city council. You have gone to the trouble of considering all the questions of audience and purpose. You have found comparative data from other libraries that make your case much more persuasive. You have assembled the whole thing into a fine presentation full of charts, graphs, and tables. Everything is going great until the mayor interrupts you to ask where you got all those numbers. You respond that they came from a state library publication that gives statistics from all the libraries in the state. Unimpressed, the mayor demands to know how you know if those statistics from the other libraries are any good. How were they collected? Are they audited? Are you sure they collected their data in the same way you did? You have no answer to these questions, and you feel the credibility you have tried so hard to build slip away.

This kind of a scenario is not uncommon, especially when you are talking to someone who doesn't like the argument you are making. When people are faced with overwhelming evidence they don't like, they often take the offensive and try to question the reliability of the evidence. When it comes to statistics, this means raising doubts about the quality of the data. If you have not yet been the victim of this type of technique, you can count yourself lucky and take a few precautions to protect your argument.

First, know the sources of any data you use. Even if you know nothing else about the data you are using, you must know where they came from. This means being able to cite a publication. If it is unpublished information obtained from another library, the state library, or some other entity, you should be able to say where you obtained the data. If you got the data from the Internet, take care to note the source (Gopher server, FTP site, Web server, etc.). And don't forget to cite the source of the data in a publication.

Second, try to find out something about how the data were obtained. Obviously, you know how your own statistics were collected and that your staff understood the definitions for each data element. Do you know as much about the library down the road or across the state? Possibly, but probably not. Other libraries might not care so much about maintaining high standards of data quality as you and your staff do. While it is no guarantee of accuracy, it is nevertheless helpful to know that all libraries will be using a common set of data definitions published by the state library. For data from other sources, try to find out the collection methodology. Were the data collected automatically or were they reported? Was it a sample and, if so, what is the margin of error? Over what period were the data collected? Is the collecting agency likely to have the expertise needed to evaluate the quality of the data? Again, the more you know about your data, the less likely you are to be taken by surprise when someone else asks you these questions.

Third, do you have reason to believe that the data you are using are inaccurate? Do the statistics seem out of line with what you expected to find? Are there aberrations in the data, such as some very high or very low numbers (known as "outliers" among statisticians), that make them incompatible with the rest of your data? Do the data disagree with the same or similar data taken from elsewhere? Have you found mathematical errors in the data? Do you have personal knowledge that the methods used to collect the data were faulty? These are all danger signs that the data you are using might be inaccurate. If you have serious doubts about the reliability of your data, don't use them. It is worse to use data that are wrong than to not use them at all. For one thing, if you use bad data and you know it, it is dishonest. For another, you will be drawing false conclusions. Finally, if the data you use are found to be flawed, your own reliability and credibility are threatened.

But you won't always know. The best you can do is pay attention to the numbers you are using. Make sure you are using the same year's data for all elements. Double-check your math. Look for things that don't seem right. If you see a number that lies far outside the rest of the data you have, or that looks wrong, or that seems to challenge or undermine your argument, investigate it. Find out which library those data are from, on what day they occurred, or who recorded them. Satisfy yourself that you understand those anomalies and outliers. Question your assumptions about the data and your conclusions. Let someone else look at it before you publish it. In short, be thoroughly comfortable about your material before you present it because you will have to answer for it and you will want to be sure you have enough of the answers to sound confident.

This is why it is doubly important to take care that the statistics that you collect and report to the state library be very accurate. It is not important only to you, but also to someone else in another library who may someday use your library's data. It is just as important to their case that your data be accurate as the accuracy of their data is to you.

PRINCIPLES OF DATA USE

There are a couple of rules to observe when it comes to using data. Although these may seem commonsensical and obvious, they are not always observed. Observing these rules will make your data presentation stronger and will contribute to a more effective overall presentation.

First, try to go beyond description to analysis. Use your data to describe what has happened at your library: how many books were checked out, how many people visited, how many reference questions were answered, how much was spent on what, and how many books were bought. This is important information, and you will want to know it and share it with others, but the time will come when you want more. Descriptive data address the "What?" question. But you will eventually need data that answer the question of "Why?" You will want to understand the causal relationships between events.

If you have observed that use of the reference collection has been declining 5% each year, don't you want to know why it has been falling off? Maybe it's because students prefer using the new high school library or because your new reference librarian is unfriendly to the public or because you changed the library hours. You probably have some ideas why, but statistical analysis may be the most effective and safest way to substantiate your hypothesis.

Second, pay attention to the quality, integrity, and relevance of your data. To paraphrase Edward Tufte, a noted statistician from Yale University: If your numbers are not interesting, you're using the wrong numbers. When you use data, it often becomes easy to get fixated on a particular notion. We may want to prove, for example, that our library is dreadfully underfunded. We gather comparative numbers, and they show that this isn't really true. Among our comparison group, we fare pretty well. So what do we do? Well, unfortunately, we may sometimes go scrounging around for ways to highlight our imagined lack of funding by tweaking our data. We might look around for a very selective comparison group, or show the numbers as means or medians or whatever looks most favorable to our argument, or maybe we graph it in such a way that our case looks better.

This is the wrong way to approach the argument. If the numbers do not support the argument, then the argument should be dropped or another way of honestly assessing the problem should be pursued. The data that are used to support an argument should be relevant to the argument, they should truly support the argument, and they should be quality data (as we have already addressed in this chapter). The further we stray from these principles, the greater the risk that we are downright lying with statistics, and the more we will be undermining our case.

A FINAL NOTE ON "LIES, DAMNED LIES, AND STATISTICS"

This discussion of using honest and relevant data brings to mind the delightfully insightful 1950s classic *How to Lie with Statistics* by Darrell Huff. The title alone has given rise to the notion (especially among those who have not read the book) that using statistics is somehow dishonest. The idea is that statistics are the perfect tool of those who would distort the truth because statistics can be manipulated to support any point. And Huff's book nicely describes how statistics can be used to present a false or misleading picture. Each of us can probably point to some firsthand observation of this type of misuse.

But the wry humor of Huff's book lies in the ironic way it turns shady practices into object lessons in how *not* to lie with statistics. It is perfectly all right to formulate a hypothesis and go looking for the data to prove it, but if you find that the data do not support your position, you have the wrong data. Change your position to fit the data rather than manipulate the data to fit the argument. Look for your argument to emerge from the data. Ultimately this will be more satisfying, more powerful, and less risky.

This doesn't mean that you can't emphasize data that will show your library in the best light. By the same token, you have no obligation to call attention to facts about your library that would be detrimental to your argument. It also does not mean that, if you use a particular statistic to say something positive about your library, you are ethically prohibited from using that same statistic in a different context to show that your library has some catching up to do. Statistics, like any other information, acquire different meaning in different contexts. If you are forty years old, your age would make you above average in a college classroom but below average in a retirement community. If you keep in mind that in either context you are still forty, and not try to represent yourself as either older or younger than you are, you are using statistics honestly.

In short, do not hesitate to use statistical data to make or support an argument because you believe that it is somehow sneaky to do so. Despite the popular notion that statistics are widely misused and suspect, people tend to find statistics more credible than almost any other form of evidence. Casey Stengel, the great baseball manager, was fond of saying "You could look it up!" to end an argument. For Stengel, like most of us, statistics are the authority, the official record, the ultimate proof. The more you work with statistics, the more you will find that it is actually much harder to lie with statistics than it is to use them to show the truth.

10 TECHNIQUES OF DATA USE

Most librarians are not statisticians. At best, our formal education in statistics usually consists of one required course taken during the MLS program. Many library school students find that required statistics course (sometimes called "research methods") completely out of place and unwelcome. Most librarians and library paraprofessionals come to the field motivated by a variety of humanistic interests: a love of books, a belief in the value of reading, a commitment to the principles of lifelong learning and citizen access to information. For the library science student, the course in statistics often seems far removed from these lofty motives and, therefore, irrelevant. And, for students whose background is liberal arts, statistics might seem like a particularly dry and boring topic.

When students get out of library school, they find that, like it or not, the library profession, like any other social service or educational profession, uses a lot of data. You, your supervisor, your library board, or your mayor want to know something about your library. You find that a body of data exists about your library and you can use that data to answer the questions you and others have about your library. If only you could remember something from that statistics course!

This chapter is a brief exploration of the basic techniques of data use. These are simple concepts and applications, which will serve the great majority of your needs. If you find you need a more sophisticated application, or your interest is piqued to pursue more complex forms of analysis, I suggest you refer to *Statistics for Library Decision Making: A Handbook*, by Peter Hernon.

PER CAPITA

For most of your data presentations, you will have to decide how you want to show your numbers. There are some instances where it will be perfectly okay to show your data as total figures; that is, you can present total circulation or total visits. This information is purely descriptive; it tells you nothing about the statistic in relation to anything else. The first step in the process of making the data relevant is to present them as per capita numbers. *Per capita* means "by individual," and it is simply an expression of how many of a particular measure there are per person in your service area. You arrive at the number by dividing the measure by the population of your legal service area. So if your annual circulation is 100,000, and you serve a population of 10,000 persons, your circulation per capita is 10.

Per capita expressions of data are important because they level the playing field, so to speak. If your collection size is 25,000 and another library's is 125,000, you might consider that theirs is a better stocked library than yours. But when you divide the collection size by the population and find that you own 3.5 items per capita compared to their 1.5 per capita, then you have to conclude the opposite—your library has the larger collection in relation to the population served. Whenever you compare your library to others, it is very important that you use per capita numbers. The only time this is not as important is when you are comparing libraries in a very narrow population range, because the population range accomplishes the same goal as the use of the per capita. Even so, you should still use per capita numbers if only because they are easier to read and understand than the total figures.

COMPARISON GROUPS

One of the most common ways library professionals use library data is to compare them to the same data from several other libraries. This group of libraries is called a *comparison group*. Most often, the aim in using a comparison group is to make the case that the library is either ahead or behind other similar libraries. If, for example, you want to increase the amount you are allocated for materials, you will want to show that your materials expenditures are at the low end of a range of other similar libraries.

Which libraries should you use? Should your group be libraries serving towns of similar size? Or should the comparison group have similar budgets? Or serve communities with similar demographic profiles? Or be located nearby? Like most data use problems, choosing a comparison group should be done thoughtfully. Partly, it will be a matter of the attitude of your audience. If your town has a history of competition with the next town over, taking a local comparison group might be a good idea. If, on the other hand, your mayor is more interested in the statewide picture, choosing a purely local comparison group would be unwise. In some cases, municipalities have a set of towns against which they routinely compare their programs.

The safest and most common comparison group—though not always the most effective or interesting—is one based on similar service area populations. It is natural to think of this first. You want to show how you compare to libraries of similar size across the state or nation. In picking a group based on population, take your population and find a range of libraries that puts your library in the middle. For example, if the population served by your library is 35,000 persons, pick a range of between 25,000 and 45,000. If this range causes the group to be too large or too small, either expand or trim it to get a sample that you are comfortable with. Avoid making cuts to your comparison group that will present your data in a more favorable light, however. Your goal should be to create a comparison group that presents an accurate picture of your library in relation to others.

Sometimes you will want to choose a sample group according to some criterion other than population. Consider, for example, that when you select a comparison group based on population, you are not taking into account the different amounts those libraries spend on services. The library that spends $65 per capita and the library that spends $10 per capita are arbitrarily thrown together though their level of service output will probably be very different for a reason that has nothing to do with population. If you are interested in comparing your library's service outputs, you might find it more helpful to compare your library with other libraries that spend a similar amount per capita. In that way, you can compare how much you get for your money and see whether you are ahead of or behind the pack.

Briefly restated, then, population groupings work best for comparisons of expenditures per capita, while groupings by expenditures per capita are a more effective way to compare service outputs. Using this logic, I produced the comparisons like the one in Figure 10-1 for every public library in Texas in 1991.

How many libraries should you use in the sample group? Ideally, you should display an equivalent number above and below your library, but if you take groupings that fall between round numbers—say, libraries serving 10,000 to 20,000 persons—this seldom works out to be the case. If you have roughly equivalent numbers above and below, count yourself lucky and go on. If your comparison group is too large or too small, however, you will have to adjust the list to a manageable length.

A comparison group that is too small will distort the effect of the data and will strike the reader as suspicious and unconvincing. A comparison group that is too large will be too hard to read, risking the chance that your point will be misunderstood. Select a range that is wide enough to give some weight to your argument, but not so large that the argument gets lost.

AVERAGE, MEAN, AND MEDIAN

These terms are often confused. Frequently, when we speak of an average, we could be referring to either the median or the mean.

Figure 10–1 Comparison Chart for Texas Public Libraries in 1991

Library: **Denton** Public Library
City: Denton

Comparison Group 1: Service Measures for Libraries with Similar Expenditures per Capita.

Library	City	Population	Exp/Cap	Items	Items/Cap	Circulation	Circ/Cap	Reference	Ref/Cap	Visits	Visits/Cap
Sterling Municipal Library	Baytown	85,269	$13.02	246,357	2.89	758,437	8.89	27,924	.33	297,203	3.49
Andrews County Library	Andrews	14,338	13.09	46,010	3.21	52,473	3.66	8,112	.57	59,680	4.16
Pilot Point Community Library	Pilot Point	3,011	13.34	15,120	5.02	28,356	9.42	10	.00	13,643	4.53
Port Arthur Public Library	Port Arthur	58,724	13.67	166,563	2.84	259,331	4.42	18,222	.31	181,344	3.09
Friona Public Library	Friona	3,688	13.68	24,086	6.53	29,517	8.00	971	.26	11,284	3.06
Denton Public Library	**Denton**	**78,614**	**13.71**	**132,101**	**1.68**	**536,383**	**6.82**	**61,621**	**.78**	**287,877**	**3.66**
Houston Public Library	Houston	1,630,553	13.79	6,470,953	3.97	6,342,340	3.89	3,793,094	2.33	4,961,502	3.04
Georgetown Public Library	Georgetown	14,842	13.79	51,726	3.49	143,124	9.64	4,576	.31	67,562	4.55
Victoria Public Library	Victoria	74,361	13.98	152,998	2.06	361,147	4.86	83,702	1.13	207,081	2.78
Effie & Wilton Hebert Public Library	Port Neches	12,974	14.13	43,354	3.34	70,523	5.44	4,886	.38	40,723	3.14
Fort Worth Public Library	Fort Worth	447,619	14.27	2,543,475	5.68	2,238,871	5.00	1,257,771	2.81	123,568	.28

Comparison Group 2: Financial Measures Compared with Libraries Serving Similar Population.

Library	City	Population	Expenditures	Exp/Cap	Mat'ls Exp	Mat'ls Exp/Cap	Salary Exp.	Libn's Salary
El Paso County Library	Fabens	66,570	$150,089	$2.25	$23,800	$.36	$112,185	$32,000
Rosenberg Library	Galveston	70,245	1,528,001	21.75	215,516	3.07	780,716	55,000
Victoria Public Library	Victoria	74,361	1,039,490	13.98	123,892	1.67	613,835	47,775
Richardson Public Library	Richardson	74,840	1,392,910	18.61	164,323	2.20	1,115,328	55,754
Tyler Public Library	Tyler	75,450	816,698	10.82	93,746	1.24	568,464	50,232
Denton Public Library	**Denton**	**78,614**	**1,077,833**	**13.71**	**145,354**	**1.85**	**781,309**	**69,095**
Sterling Municipal Library	Baytown	85,269	1,110,254	13.02	117,713	1.38	783,528	55,701
Carrollton Public Library	Carrollton	90,020	1,129,101	12.54	160,994	1.79	763,753	52,200
Longview Public Library	Longview	90,749	821,536	9.05	138,711	1.53	561,868	45,000
Kemp Public Library	Wichita Falls	96,259	640,154	6.65	137,207	1.43	377,720	35,582
Tom Green County Library System	San Angelo	98,458	884,492	8.98	185,786	1.89	614,295	36,000

"#N/A!", "#Value!" = zero or no value in equation
(1) = missing data from library

Produced by the Library Development Division, Texas State Library
Source of data: Texas Public Library Statistics for 1991

The *average* is the same as the *mean*. It refers to the sum of a series of numbers divided by the number in the series. Take, for example, the following hypothetical series of directors' salaries:

$12,000
$19,000
$21,450
$30,800
$33,500
$35,000
$37,200
$41,000
$45,000
$57,000
$88,000

To get the average, or mean, add all 11 numbers together (the total is $419,950), then divide by the number of salaries in the group (11); the resulting average, or mean, is $38,178 (rounded up to the nearest dollar).

The *median* is the number in the middle. Finding the median in a small range like the one above is pretty easy. You simply put the salaries in order from lowest to highest as they are shown, and find the salary that has the same number of cases above and below it. In the group of 11 library directors' salaries above, it is easy to find the median by finding the salary with 5 above and 5 below. The median in this group is $35,000. The median is also known as the 50th percentile. If there are an even number of cases in your group, the median is the average of the two numbers in the middle.

In the above example, the mean and the median are pretty close together because the sample is more or less evenly distributed. In some cases, however, you will find that the median and the mean are very different numbers. Take, for example, this range of circulation per capita figures:

3.52
3.75
4.14
4.44
4.71
4.95
5.07
5.26
6.45
9.65
18.77

The mean, or average, for these numbers is 6.42, but the median is only 4.95, a rather significant variance from the mean—1.47 circulations per capita. Why the big difference? Because of those two figures at the high end of the range: 9.65 and 18.77. Numbers that vary greatly from the rest in the range tend to skew the average of those numbers. Sometimes this is corrected for by throwing out, or not using, the highest and lowest numbers in a range. If we applied this method to the range of numbers above, our mean would drop to 5.38, a figure much closer to the median. If we want to show all the numbers and not let the unrepresentative highs and lows distort our characterization of our group as a whole, however, we would choose to talk about the median. You can tell just by looking at the figures in this group, the median (4.95 circs per capita) is much more representative of the range than the average. In most cases, you will find that the median is more descriptive and accurate than the average. Nevertheless, there will be times when you will also want or need to use the average. Whether you use the median or the mean (average), be sure always to clearly label your statistics so that your audience will know what you are presenting.

PERCENTILES

Percentiles, sometimes referred to as "normative values," or "norms," can be a handy way to characterize a large amount of data. For example, several states publish tables that show all the normative values for all the libraries in the state in particular measures. This makes it much easier to see characteristics of the state as a whole than would be possible by staring at a table of figures for the hundreds of libraries in the state.

Percentile refers to the position of an individual case relative to the percent of cases below it. Remember that I said that the median is the same as the 50th percentile and that the median comes in the middle of the range? That means that half—or 50%—of the individual cases in the range lie below the median. Thus the 25th percentile means the number below which 25% of the cases occur, the 75th percentile is the number below which 75% of the cases occur. To be specific, if we divide our table to show every tenth percentile, we are showing *deciles*, if we show every 25th percentile, we are showing *quartiles*.

Figure 10-2 is one of a series of tables produced by the Texas State Library. The table shows the quartiles for a series of measures of library service. Any librarian in the state can use the table to locate her library in its population grouping on the table to learn how its performance compares to other similar-sized libraries in the state.

Figure 10–2 Percentile Table

Table 5 - Items per Capita

Population	Number of Libraries	Low	25th %ile	50th %ile	75th %ile	High	Average
Under 2,000	48	0.85	5.33	9.04	14.59	48.11	11.28
2,000–4,999	116	1.91	3.60	5.14	6.15	12.33	5.15
5,000-9,999	105	0.67	2.42	2.98	4.04	27.64	3.50
10,000-14,999	49	0.99	1.85	2.48	3.23	5.82	2.63
15,000-24,999	48	0.69	1.57	2.13	2.75	4.66	2.24
25,000-49,999	48	0.44	1.44	1.73	2.14	3.09	1.77
50,000-99,999	19	0.73	1.10	1.39	1.72	4.19	1.58
100,000-249,999	17	0.50	0.84	1.16	1.37	2.15	1.20
Over 250,000	7	0.36	0.57	0.64	0.87	1.77	0.81
State Total	457	0.36	1.85	2.92	4.96	48.11	4.12

Note: Total items (from 1993 AR/SMA question 38 "Volumes, Items, or Physical Units") divided by population served.

RANKING

Ranking is one of the simplest and most powerful ways to display a range of data. Ranking means sorting a series of numbers in either decreasing or increasing order. While you will sometimes use reverse-order ranking (least to most), you will probably most often find a ranking that puts the largest item first. This is the ranking scheme with which we are most familiar, though you can also sort your data in ascending order so that the smallest value is at the top and largest at the bottom. When we say that Chicago is the third largest city in the United States, we mean that in rank order it falls third, behind New York and Los Angeles.

Let's take a look at how ranking data can yield important information. Figure 10-3 shows a set of libraries with their population served and expenditures per capita:

Figure 10–3 Chart Sorted Alphabetically		
Library	**Population Served**	**Expenditures per Capita ($)**
Azteca Public Library	8,871	10.53
Carmello County Library	11,635	9.74
Castle Hill Public Library	9,894	14.85
Evitas Public Library	4,578	12.17
Jeffrey Regional Library District	19,452	10.44
Jovita Free Public Library	10,567	10.33
Kerbey Public Library	3,857	13.56
Shady Grove Public Library	3,264	11.02
Threadgill County Library	15,712	8.29

This alphabetical arrangement by library is helpful for finding the name of the library but makes it hard to draw any conclusions about the library data.

The table in Figure 10-4 displays the same data sorted by population.

Figure 10–4 Chart Sorted by Population		
Library	**Population Served**	**Expenditure per Capita ($)**
Jeffrey Regional Library District	19,452	10.44
Threadgill County Library	15,712	8.29
Carmello County Library	11,635	9.74
Jovita Free Public Library	10,567	10.33
Castle Hill Public Library	9,894	14.85
Azteca Public Library	8,871	10.53
Evitas Public Library	4,578	12.17
Kerbey Public Library	3,857	13.56
Shady Grove Public Library	3,264	11.02

The display in Figure 10-4 makes a little more sense. It at least shows us the rank order of the libraries by population served. But the point of the chart is to compare expenditure per capita, and this display makes those data hard to see. We'd like to arrange it in rank order by expenditure per capita as shown in Figure 10-5.

Figure 10–5 Chart Sorted by Expenditure per Capita		
Library	Population Served	Expenditures per Capita ($)
Castle Hill Public Library	9,894	14.85
Kerbey Public Library	3,857	13.56
Evitas Public Library	4,578	12.17
Shady Grove Public Library	3,264	11.02
Azteca Public Library	8,871	10.53
Jeffrey Regional Library District	19,452	10.44
Jovita Free Public Library	10,567	10.33
Carmello County Library	11,635	9.74
Threadgill County Library	15,712	8.29

Now that's even better, because now we can see that Castle Hill Library spends the most per capita and Threadgill County spends the least. But this still isn't good enough. We want to see the relationship between the rank orders. The way we do that is with a presentation as shown in Figure 10-6.

Figure 10–6 Presentation Chart with Rankings Shown				
Library	Population Served	Rank	Expenditures per Capita ($)	Rank
Jeffrey Regional Library District	19,452	1	10.44	6
Threadgill County Library	15,712	2	8.29	9
Carmello County Library	11,635	3	9.74	8
Jovita Free Public Library	10,567	4	10.33	7
Castle Hill Public Library	9,894	5	14.85	1
Azteca Public Library	8,871	6	10.53	5
Evitas Public Library	4,578	7	12.17	3
Kerbey Public Library	3,857	8	13.56	2
Shady Grove Public Library	3,264	9	11.02	4

In Figure 10-6, we have added two columns to the chart, one showing the rank order of the libraries by the population served and the other that shows the rank order of expenditures per capita. Now we see a pattern emerge here that we could not see before. We see that for several of the larger libraries, expenditures per capita are not consistent with the population ranking. The director of Threadgill County Library could now make an effective argument for more funding by demonstrating that the library serves the second largest service area with the lowest per capita expenditures in the region.

When you compare your library to other libraries, one of your first considerations should be to sort your data. It is very easy to do with most spreadsheet softwares, and it can reveal some surprising and convincing information.

MULTIVARIATE ANALYSIS

Multivariate is a term used by statisticians to mean statistical displays that show multiple variables simultaneously—that is, more than one series of data at the same time. If, for example, your data simultaneously tracks income per capita and expenditures per capita, or perhaps materials per capita and circulation per capita, it is multivariate. Using multivariate data allows you more easily to discover and demonstrate causal relationships. For this reason, generally speaking, multivariate data are more descriptive and more interesting than data that contain only one series. Figure 10-6 exemplifies multivariate analysis.

TIME SERIES

A statistical technique that you will probably want to use often is the *time series* (also known as a "longitudinal series"). As the name implies, a *time series* tracks a given statistic at regular intervals over a period of time. This is a very common, widely used technique of descriptive statistics. And it is the only way to study progression over time. Do you recall our discussion of benchmarking in the last chapter? Any time you wish to measure the progress of a particular library activity against a benchmark, you will have to use a time series.

To demonstrate the idea of time series (and a few others along the way), let's take a look at an imaginary figure for your hypothetical library. Folks visited your library—we'll call it the Snakebite Public Library and make you the director—at a rate of 6.2 per capita last year (1994). You can't tell much about that number by itself. Is it high or low? Who knows? For it to have much meaning, you have to show it in some context. First you look to the other libraries in the county. You go to the statistical report published annually by the state library and you assemble this table (Figure 10-7):

Figure 10–7 Dry Gulch County Libraries (1994) Chart	
Library Name	**Visits per Capita**
Snakebite P.L.	6.2
Dry Gulch P.L.	7.5
Saddlebags P.L.	8.1
Caprock P.L.	8.2
Dusty Trail P.L.	9.6

Figure 10-7 is a little better. Now you can see that you have the lowest visits per capita of any of those libraries. But you want to know more. You want to know how those numbers have changed over the past several years. You go back to the state library statistical publications for the last five years and create the time series shown in Figure 10-8.

Figure 10–8 Dry Gulch County Libraries (1990–1994) Chart 1					
Library Name	**Visits per Capita**				
	1990	**1991**	**1992**	**1993**	**1994**
Snakebite P.L.	4.7	5.2	5.4	5.8	6.2
Dry Gulch P.L.	7.1	6.9	7.4	7.3	7.5
Saddlebags P.L.	7.3	7.4	7.6	7.9	8.1
Caprock P.L.	7.7	7.9	8.0	8.2	8.2
Dusty Trail P.L.	9.0	9.1	9.6	9.5	9.6

Now you can see a pattern emerging, one that you might not have expected. Yes, visits per capita for the Snakebite Library are low for 1994, but look how far you've come since 1990. Compare the difference between Snakebite Public and Dusty Trail Public in 1990 and again in 1994. See the difference? Your library is closing the gap. This point would not have emerged without running a time series.

You can now emphasize your finding by one further addition to the table.

Figure 10–9 Dry Gulch County Libraries (1990–1994) Chart 2						
Library Name	**Visits per Capita**					
	1990	**1991**	**1992**	**1993**	**1994**	**% change 1990 to 1994**
Snakebite P.L.	4.7	5.2	5.4	5.8	6.2	31.9%
Dry Gulch P.L.	7.1	6.9	7.4	7.3	7.5	5.6%
Saddlebags P.L.	7.3	7.4	7.6	7.9	8.1	11.0%
Caprock P.L.	7.7	7.9	8.0	8.2	8.2	6.5%
Dusty Trail P.L.	9.0	9.1	9.6	9.5	9.6	6.7%

Figure 10-9 adds a column showing the percent change from 1990 to 1994 (figured by subtracting the 1990 figure from the 1994 figure, then dividing the product by the 1990 figure). This column demonstrates at a glance the dramatic rate of increase for visits per capita at the Snakebite Public Library compared to other libraries in Dry Gulch County. The message that you would likely drive home with this chart is, "We've come a long way, but we must do more to try to catch up."

Remember that your goal is not just to describe what has happened, but to try to show why it has happened. To that end, let's develop our table a bit further in search of a possible explanation of why our visits per capita have climbed so dramatically. You might suspect, for example, that the amount you have spent on materials has begun to pay off with increased usage. So you go back and fill out your display with the per capita amounts spent for materials during the same five-year period. Now your chart will look something like Figure 10-10.

Figure 10–10 Dry Gulch County Libraries (1990–1994) Chart 3						
Visits per Capita						
Library Name	**1990**	**1991**	**1992**	**1993**	**1994**	**% change**
Snakebite P.L.	4.7	5.2	5.4	5.8	6.2	31.9%
Dry Gulch P.L.	7.1	6.9	7.4	7.3	7.5	5.6%
Saddlebags P.L.	7.3	7.4	7.6	7.9	8.1	11.0%
Caprock P.L.	7.7	7.9	8.0	8.2	8.2	6.5%
Dusty Trail P.L.	9.0	9.1	9.6	9.5	9.6	6.7%
Expenditures per Capita						
Snakebite P.L.	2.3	2.7	3.0	3.3	3.3	43.5%
Dry Gulch P.L.	3.1	3.3	3.6	3.4	3.3	6.5%
Saddlebags P.L.	3.7	3.9	4.0	3.9	4.1	10.8%
Caprock P.L.	3.4	3.6	3.7	3.7	3.7	8.8%
Dusty Trail P.L.	4.3	4.4	4.5	4.5	4.6	7.0%

Now you have suggested that the increase in expenditures for materials resulted in increased attendance. The argument seems like commonsense marketing: an improved collection brings more people into the library. Except for two problems.

First, the table does not actually demonstrate that increased expenditures have resulted in increased usage. To do this, you would have to show that visits were pretty low until you started spending more money on the collection. So you go back several years prior to the time you increased collection expenditures. At this point, by the way, we can drop the comparison table, focus on the movement between the variables for the Snakebite Public Library alone, and thereby greatly simplify the table to something like Figure 10–11.

Figure 10–11 Snakebite Public Library Chart								
	1987	**1988**	**1989**	**1990**	**1991**	**1992**	**1993**	**1994**
Visits per Capita	3.7	3.9	3.8	4.7	5.2	5.4	5.8	6.2
Matls. Exp. per Capita	1.7	1.6	2.1	2.3	2.7	3.0	3.3	3.3

This table shows that there does indeed seem to be a relationship between visits per capita and expenditures per capita. We say this because when expenditures per capita increased in 1989, visits per capita—which had been static—increased sharply in the following year, 1990.

The second problem is whether we really know that the extra amount spent on the collection caused the visits per capita to increase as we have suggested, or whether the greater usage was caused by another factor that we have not considered. Perhaps the library added staff, or maybe hours were expanded. Trying to determine cause-and-effect relationships from two sets of data brings us to another series of elementary statistical concepts that you can add to your tool kit: correlation, cross-tabulation, and multiple regression.

CORRELATION, MULTIPLE REGRESSION, AND CROSS-TABULATION

Correlation refers to relations that exist between two or more series of data. As we have said, the goal of any sort of research is to try to demonstrate causal relationships between various phenomena.

In the last section, we explored a fictional case that suggested a causal relationship—or correlation—between the higher amounts spent on the collection and the increase in library visits per capita. Note that I used the word "suggested" rather than "proved." Unfortunately, using statistical data alone, it cannot be said unequivocally that the relation is absolutely true. All we can say is that there seems to be a correlation between the higher expenditures and the increased visits. Researchers describe correlation in terms of prediction. One situation can be said to predict another because there is a high correlation between the presence of one and the presence of the other. Then we make a logical inference as to which situation is the cause and which the effect. We have inferred a causal relation between these two phenomena. For most purposes, this will probably be enough.

Professional statisticians would want to know much more about this relationship, and sometimes you will, too. To state confidently that there is a causal relationship between the expenditures and the visits, you have to eliminate the effect of any other factors. To do this requires a more sophisticated method known as *multiple regression*, which you will rarely, if ever, need to use. To identify more accurately causal relationships between circumstances, statistical researchers systematically eliminate all variables in order to find those which are the most reliable predictors of the outcome. This technique of systematically backing out—or regressing—all the variables to look for causal relationships is called multiple regression. This is a complicated process beyond the scope of this book. Isolating variables will also usually prove to be difficult, if not impossible, especially if only one library facility is in the study.

It usually is not necessary for you to perform such elaborate procedures as multiple regression in order to learn something interesting about your data. If you are searching for correlations and patterns in larger data sets with a number of variables, another technique, *cross-tabulation* (or *cross-tab*, for short), can be very useful. Cross-tab tables show relationships between two or more independent variables. They are used to organize raw data into groupings by any element in the group.

Creating a cross-tabulation table by hand is difficult and time-consuming, especially if you don't have an idea what pattern you are looking for. Fortunately, most commercial data base and spreadsheet programs (such as EXCEL, LOTUS, dBASE, and QUATTRO PRO) will perform automatic cross-tab analysis and display of data bases. This can be a very handy way to look for relationships in your data without spending hours number crunching with a calculator.

ADJUSTING DATA

One final concept that you should understand when working with data in time series is the concept of adjusting data. There are any number of ways in which data can be adjusted, but this discussion focuses on adjusting financial data for inflation because this is by far the most common type of adjustment that you will have to make on your data.

Adjusting for inflation is a commonly understood practice and one that you have probably frequently encountered in newspaper and magazine tables and graphs. The idea is that if you are comparing, say, expenditures in 1995 with expenditures in 1990, the number of dollars spent is not comparable because the steadily rising cost of most goods and services—inflation—makes the 1990 dollars worth more than the 1995 dollars. In an inflationary economy, chances are the number of dollars spent (also known as absolute dollars) in a given year will be greater than the number spent several years before. But knowing the absolute dollars spent does not tell us what we really want to know—that is, What is the relative buying power of those dollars now and then? Sure, we spent more in 1995 than in 1990, but could we buy as much or more now as then or is our buying power actually decreasing?

To find out, we have to adjust the absolute dollars for inflation. How do we do that? With a device known as a *price index*, which measures the rate of inflation by tracking the increase in price of a specific set of goods and services at intervals against a given reference period. For the base reference period, the index will be set at 100 and—assuming there is inflation—each interval after the base period will be a number higher than 100 that shows the percentage increase since the base reference period. So, if the index is 100 in the first year and 103 at the end of the second year, then the annual rate of inflation for those specific items is 3%.

This is the basic idea of the Consumer Price Index, or CPI, published by the Bureau of Labor Statistics of the U.S. Department of Labor. The base period for the current index was 1982-1984. By the end of May of 1993, the average price index for all regions of the United States was 144.2. This tells us that the rate of inflation was 44.2% between the base period 1982-1984 and May 1993.

Simple, right? Well, not exactly. In the first place, things cost different amounts in different parts of the country. Anyone who has ever moved from the Midwest to the Northeast knows that the price of a house in Connecticut is much higher than that of a comparable one in Nebraska. So a price index in Nebraska will not be valid in Connecticut. Then, you have to ask what goods and services are being indexed. An index of food prices is not going to be of much interest to someone trying to adjust dollars spent on transportation. You can see where this is going: There isn't just one Consumer Price Index; there are many, broken down by city, by region, and by specific types of goods and services. The figures referenced above are for all goods and services and averaged across all areas of the country.

You could adjust your financial data using the overall CPI figure, but that number reflects changes in the price of all sorts of things that the library will never purchase. It would be better to adjust your data using an index of items relevant to libraries. Fortunately, such indexes do exist. A group called Research Associates of Washington publishes an annual volume that is now called *Inflation Measures for Schools, Colleges, and Libraries*. This valuable list of inflation measures is reprinted a year later in *The Bowker Annual: Library and Book Trade Almanac*. Unfortunately for public librarians, that information is specifically geared toward school and academic libraries, but Research Associates is currently preparing an index of public library inflation that will be available for use after the end of 1995.

Once you have your index numbers, all that remains is to apply them to your expenditure data. Here's how you do that. First, take a series of expenditures data for a five-year period, as shown in Figure 10-12.

Figure 10–12 Financial Data Chart 1					
	1989	**1990**	**1991**	**1992**	**1993**
Expenditures ($)	125,000	135,000	140,000	147,000	150,000

Then put in another row for the index figures (Figure 10-13). For this example, we can use the CPI for all items averaged over all regions.

Figure 10–13 Financial Data Chart 2					
	1989	**1990**	**1991**	**1992**	**1993**
Expenditures ($)	125,000	135,000	140,000	147,000	150,000
CPI	126.1	133.8	137.9	141.9	145.8

What you do next is find the change in the inflation index from one year to the next, expressed as the percentage of change. But instead of expressing this as a percentage, you want to express it as a number greater or less than one. So you divide one year by the following year. So, for example, you would divide 126.1 by 133.8 and arrive at the number 0.9424514 (the further we carry out the decimal, the more accurate our adjustment will be). Let's continue the line, dividing the 1989 index value (126.1) by the index for each successive year. Figure 10-14 adds a line for the change in CPI against the 1989 index, which will later become the factor of adjustment.

Figure 10–14 Financial Chart 3					
	1989	**1990**	**1991**	**1992**	**1993**
Expenditures ($)	125,000	135,000	140,000	147,000	150,000
CPI	126.1	133.8	137.9	141.9	145.8
Factor	1.0	0.9424514	0.9144307	0.8886540	0.8648834

To complete the process, we multiply the actual dollars by the percentage of change in the CPI. That is, we multiply $135,000 by 0.9424514 to get $131,388. Figure 10-15 now shows our table with the added line for adjusted dollars.

Figure 10–15 Financial Data Chart 4					
	1989	1990	1991	1992	1993
Expenditures ($)	125,000	135,000	140,000	147,000	150,000
CPI	126.1	133.8	137.9	141.9	145.8
Factor	1.0	0.9424514	0.9144307	0.8886540	0.8648834
Adjusted dollars	125,000	127,231	128,020	130,632	129,733

Now we have successfully adjusted our absolute dollars for inflation. In this way, we can see that our 1993 dollars are worth only $129,733 1989 dollars. Now we can speak of the relative buying power of dollars over several years. We can clearly see from this table that while absolute expenditures have increased steadily over this five-year period, the actual buying power has remained virtually flat.

You should adjust financial data for inflation whenever you are comparing two or more years. Time series financial data not adjusted for inflation is nearly meaningless. Whenever you show absolute dollars, adjusted dollars, or both, you should clearly label the data to indicate the kind of figures displayed.

11 CHARTS AND GRAPHS

Visual displays of statistical data have become so common that charts are nearly synonymous with statistics. We have so thoroughly come to expect graphs that sometimes we are disappointed when we confront a table of numbers rather than a chart. (I have used the terms *chart* and *graph* interchangeably to refer to a visual representation of numerical data; *table* refers to the data themselves arranged in columns and rows.) Frequently we seem to rely on charts more as a visual element to jazz up our publications and presentations than as a source of information. And while charts can be an incredibly useful format for data presentation, they are not always the best format. For small data sets (fewer than ten or fifteen data elements), a table is usually preferable to a chart because it is more straightforward. Sometimes a graphic representation is the only effective way to present data. This is especially true when presenting large amounts of data in a limited space.

It is no accident that these days, when the average person is forced to consume and process huge amounts of information, that graphic arrays of data have emerged as the medium of choice for the display of quantitative information. The goal of graphic representation is—or at least should be—to allow the reader to grasp the essence of the presentation quickly and easily and move on. A graph should be designed to make it as easy as possible for the viewer to see the point you are making without digression or distraction. In a word, a graphic presentation should be elegant.

Unfortunately, we daily encounter graphics in presentations, newspapers, magazines, newsletters, and other publications that are far from elegant. At best, poorly designed charts are distracting and confusing and detract from the argument they are trying to make. At worst, they misrepresent and distort data, sometimes intentionally.

Edward Tufte, a professor of statistics and political science at Yale University, has written two fine books on the art of graphical representation of data: *The Visual Display of Quantitative Information* and *Envisioning Information*. These books have contributed, perhaps more than any other work, to the art and science of turning numerical data into pictures. Tufte rails against cluttered, cartoony charts that attempt to overcome a paucity of substance with an overabundance of decoration, ending ultimately in distortion and obfuscation of the data themselves. While Tufte is something of a dogmatist in the area of graphing data, his arguments for simple, straightforward presentations are hard to counter. Time spent browsing Tufte's beautiful books will repay you manyfold both in solid technical instruction and in inspiration, but for now, consider the following passage from *The Visual Display of Quantitative Information* (p. 15):

> Excellence in statistical graphics consists of complex ideas communicated with clarity, precision, and efficiency. Graphical displays should
> - show the data
> - induce the viewer to think about the substance rather than about methodology, graphic design, the technology of graphic production, or something else
> - avoid distorting what the data have to say
> - present many numbers in a small space
> - make larger data sets coherent
> - encourage the eye to compare different pieces of data
> - reveal the data at several levels of detail, from a broad overview to the fine structure
> - serve a reasonably clear purpose: description, exploration, tabulation, or decoration
> - be closely integrated with the statistical and verbal descriptions of a data set.

Keep Tufte's advice in mind when turning library statistics into graphics.

Before asking what data to graph and what kind of graph to use, the first and most important question you want to ask is, why do I want to graph the data? Is it because you have spotted a trend or identified a situation that can be fully described only with a graph? Or do you want a graph because a graph would relieve the tedium of a page of print? If it is the latter, don't jump to the conclusion that you should not create a graph after all. Setting all informational considerations aside for the moment, part of your goal is to create a presentation that people will read. If your graph leads to a more approachable design, your presentation will be easier to read and the graph will probably help your cause. So much the better if your graph also makes your presentation look more professional even if it reiterates a point made in the narrative text.

If you don't need the chart for your graphic design, then make an honest decision about whether a graph really contributes to your argument, or whether a table would serve just as well.

Let's assume for the sake of this chapter that a graph is the best way to show your data and that it conveys information that cannot be shown so persuasively in a table. You then have to decide what kind of graph you are going to create. There are many types of graphs that can be used, but many of these will not be suitable for your purposes. This chapter discusses several common types of graphs and charts, how to create them, what they can and can't tell you, and tips for making them more effective.

BAR CHARTS

Bar charts are often the default mode of graphic representation of simple data sets. You will probably find that bar charts will serve the majority of your needs for graphic displays. For most types of library statistical displays, bar charts will be quite sufficient and, when used sensibly, will nicely serve Tufte's goals for graphic display. Bar charts present at one glance a series of data and the relationship among series of data. Take, for instance, Figure 11-1, showing total circulation figures for a library for the years 1994 and 1995.

Figure 11–1 Circulation Figures												
	Jan	Feb	Mar	Apr	May	Jun	Jul	Aug	Sep	Oct	Nov	Dec
1994	4,992	5,254	6,408	6,772	5,490	5,583	5,691	5,339	5,892	6,203	5,641	4,528
1995	5,366	5,852	7,369	7,639	6,472	7,320	7,176	5,694	6,494	6,372	5,911	5,010

If you are like most readers, you will have to study these numbers for quite a few seconds or minutes before any patterns begin to emerge. Figure 11-2 uses a simple bar graph to present the same data.

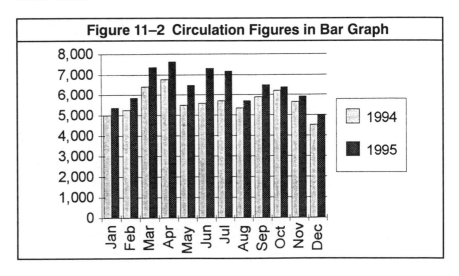

Figure 11–2 Circulation Figures in Bar Graph

Now we can see those patterns at a glance. First, we notice that in every single month of 1995, circulation is higher than that month in 1994. Second, we can see a very clear pattern of busy months and slower months. For example, note how the spring months in each year have the highest circulation; there is a smaller peak during the fall months; and use seems to fall off in the months of August, December, and January (this likely confirms observations of the staff, but the library board will probably find it interesting). Third, we can spot the areas where deviation between the years is occurring, mainly in the months of June and July. Thus, at a glance, Figure 11-2 has made apparent several things that we could not see so easily looking at the table, but this chart can be improved. The version presented in Figure 11-3 is more meaningful. It has been simplified by changing the months to one-letter designations, by changing the increments along the y-axis from 1,000 to 2,000 units, and by deemphasizing those numbers by showing them in a smaller font. The grid behind the bars has been eliminated so that all that we are left with are the x- and y-axes.

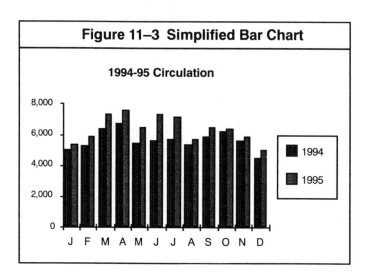

Figure 11–3 Simplified Bar Chart

One more question remains apparent: What is going on with that big increase in circulation from 1994 to 1995 during June and July? In 1994, they weren't particularly busy, but in 1995 those months jumped to among the busiest of the year. What happened? It turns out that the library introduced a summer reading club program in 1995 that had not existed in 1994. This is very important information and well worth highlighting; it can be done on the chart as shown in Figure 11-4.

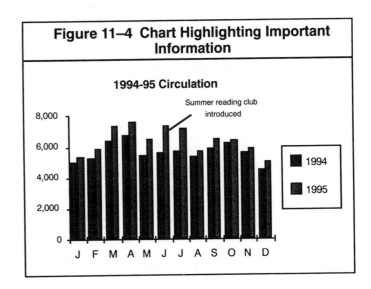

Figure 11–4 Chart Highlighting Important Information

This very sensible, straightforward graphic representation will make sense in any presentation, annual report, or public relations document.

I would advise you to declare this chart finished. But if you use any of a number of standard spreadsheet programs, you will have at your disposal the ability to create many fancy variations on this chart. If you are like me, you will be tempted to use these at least sometimes, because, after all, they are so attractive. Some of these are merely unnecessary or inappropriate; others are quite ill advised in almost any situation. In the harmless but unnecessary category, you could put the horizontal bar chart, which turns the above chart into something like Figure 11-5.

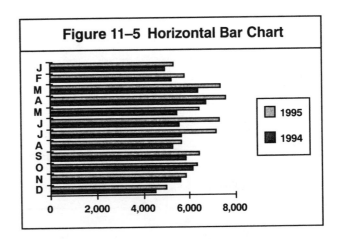

Figure 11–5 Horizontal Bar Chart

There's not much wrong with this chart other than that it adds nothing to our display. In some cases, for instance when you have longer labels along the y-axis, this type of display might be easier to read.

Figure 11-6, taken from a publication of the Utah State Library, takes clever advantage of the structure of the bar chart. The technique, used first by Keith Curry Lance of the Library Research Center at the Colorado State Library, uses the bars projecting left from the central y-axis (usually reserved for negative numbers), to present data of highly dissimilar scale to the right-hand bars. Thus a single chart is used to show extremely small and large data:

Figure 11–6 Bar Chart from Utah State Library

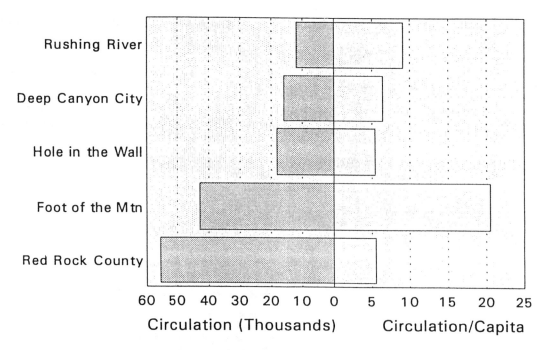

Color Country Region Libraries
Circulation and Circulation Per Capita

Data from Utah Fictitious Library Service 1993

But other uses are not so clever and tend to distract and distort more than they enhance and elucidate. To this category of dubious graphs belongs the three-dimensional bar chart, a staple of business presentations, which looks like Figure 11-7.

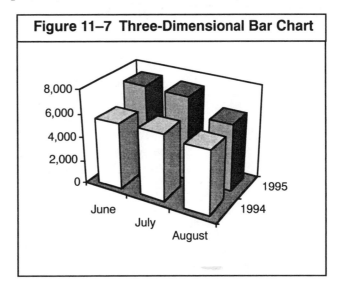

Figure 11–7 Three-Dimensional Bar Chart

The problems with this presentation are numerous. First, you can't easily tell where the tops of the bars are in relation to the axis. Second, the relative heights of the bars are difficult to gauge. For example, the values for the August bars in the above chart are much closer than they appear because the height of the 1995 bar is exaggerated by the tilt of the chart, as you can see by comparing the 3-D treatment to this two-dimensional version of the same data (Figure 11-8).

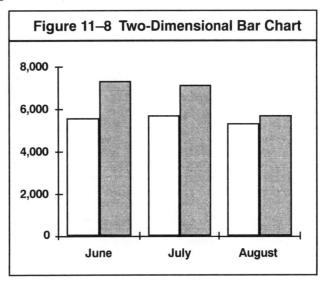

Figure 11–8 Two-Dimensional Bar Chart

Finally, the presentation says much more about the sophistication of the computer program than about the data. You will safely avoid the temptation to add useless window dressing to your charts if you keep in mind the simple rule that three-dimensional displays should be reserved for data that have three dimensions. Display two-dimensional data with a bar chart.

STACKED BARS

The stacked bar chart can be very useful in some displays. This device is most successfully used to show the relation of two parts to a whole in a series of charts. For example, say you want to show the trend of in-library use, but you want to divide this use between electronic and print resources in the reference collection. Your stacked bar chart might look like Figure 11-9.

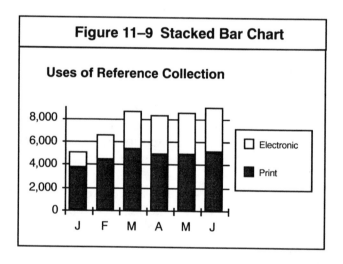

You can see the value of this kind of display in simultaneously demonstrating the relation between two parts to one another and to the total. In the above example, we can see at a glance that while in-house use of print resources forms the base and majority of uses, electronic use grew rapidly during the period.

POINT-AND-LINE CHARTS

Another extremely popular chart type—one you are probably very familiar with and that you may have used already—is the point-and-line chart, also known as a line plot. The point-and-line chart graphs data in exactly the same way as a bar chart, but instead of representing the data by columns, the data are represented by points (or plots) which are connected by a line. The earlier bar chart demonstrating circulation could easily be redrawn as the point-and-line chart shown in Figure 11-10.

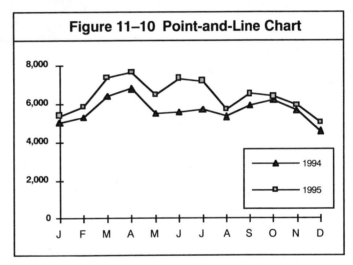

Figure 11–10 Point-and-Line Chart

As you can see, the line focuses the eye on the upward or downward movement of the lines as well as variations between the lines. For this reason, the point-and-line chart is particularly useful when you want to draw the viewer's attention to the movement between data points.

The point-and-line technique can also be used in combination with a bar chart. The contrast of the lines moving against the background of the bars highlights the contrast in movement of two similar series of data. For an example of this, we can return for a moment to our discussion from the last chapter on expenditure data adjusted for inflation. Figure 11-11 is a graphic demonstration of the data contained in Figure 10-15 from Chapter 10. Here is the relation between absolute dollars (represented by the bars) and inflation-adjusted dollars (represented by the line).

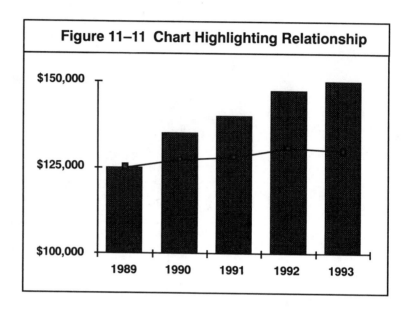

The line calls attention to the contrast between the bar and the line. It also highlights the movement of the inflation-adjusted dollars which, in this case, is much flatter than the upward trend of the absolute dollars.

AREA GRAPH

A variant of the point-and-line graph is the area graph. In an area graph, the space beneath the line is solid. This is most useful when the data show the portions of the whole represented by various elements. This is similar to the stacked bar chart. Consider, for example, the breakout of circulation by type of materials shown in Figure 11-12.

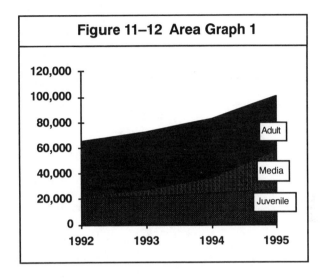

This example demonstrates a distortion inherent in this format. At first glance, adult circulation seems to be increasing. A closer look, however, will show that the only area of the collection showing any robust growth in circulation is media. Both adult and juvenile circulation are relatively flat. This distortion could be corrected by moving adult circulation to the bottom level as shown in Figure 11-13.

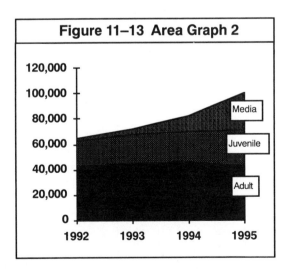

This figure is a more accurate picture of the relative movement of different parts of the collection. Instead of increasing, adult circulation is clearly shown to have actually decreased slightly in 1995.

PIE CHARTS

Pie charts are extremely popular in media as well as many of our library displays. For all their popularity, however, pie charts are generally denounced by experts in graphic displays of data. Tufte goes so far as to say that they "should never be used" (*Visual Display*, p. 178), and the French statistician Jacques Bertin declares them "completely useless" (*Graphics and Graphic Information Processing*, p. 111 [quoted in *Visual Display*, 178]). The complaint is that pie charts can represent only small data sets and that they cannot order the data in any meaningful way.

These criticisms may be valid; nevertheless, the pie chart continues to be a popular way to demonstrate the relation of parts to the whole. Pies are often used in library work to show parts of the collection, categories of income and expenditure, staffing composition, and so on. Consider, for example, a pie chart such as Figure 11-14, which demonstrates the division of the area of a building by function.

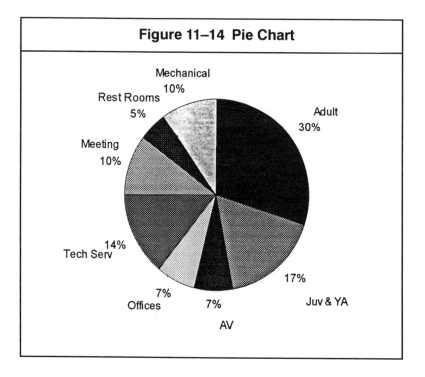

Figure 11–14 Pie Chart

And the experts will tell you to avoid cutaways—that is, pulling out one wedge of the pie, as pictured in Figure 11-15.

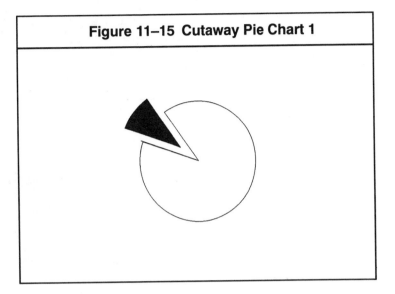

Figure 11–15 Cutaway Pie Chart 1

But if you feel compelled to do a cutaway from a pie chart, the best kind would be for a subset of one or more logically grouped elements. To go back to our example of building space distribution by function (Figure 11-14), we might do a cutaway of the office and technical services areas, as shown in Figure 11-16.

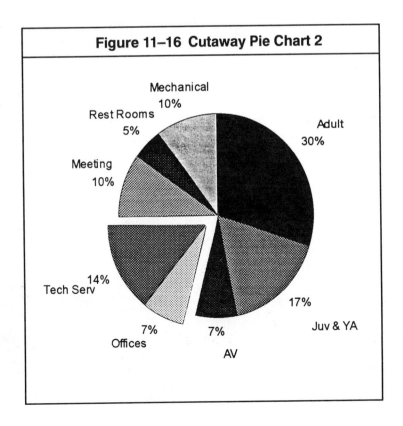

Figure 11–16 Cutaway Pie Chart 2

But just as I urged you to pass up the 3-D bar chart, I would recommend that you avoid using the bell-and-whistle capabilities of your software to produce a 3-D pie chart, such as Figure 11-17.

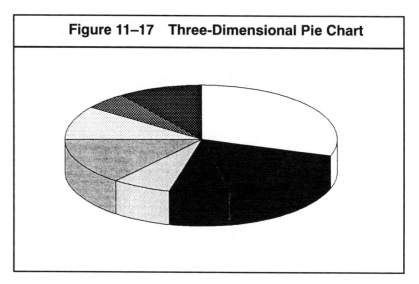

Figure 11–17   Three-Dimensional Pie Chart

The three-dimensional projection of this pie adds nothing to the presentation and creates a foreshortening effect that distorts the only real value of the pie chart—that is, relative values represented by relative areas. If, however, you believe that the 3-D pie is important to your presentation, at least minimize the degree of backward tilt so that the effect of the distortion is limited, as shown in Figure 11-18.

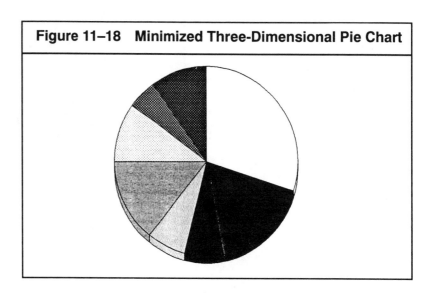

Figure 11–18   Minimized Three-Dimensional Pie Chart

SCATTERPLOTS

Scatterplots are a type of graphic display you will probably rarely use, but they may occasionally come in handy. To understand fully the significance of scatterplots, you should refer back to the discussion of correlation in Chapter 10. You will remember that correlation is the coincidence of circumstances that occurs in such a way that we can infer a relationship between those circumstances. You can think of scatterplot as the graphic display that describes correlation. In creating a scatter diagram, you plot one set of data for a group of subjects along one axis and a second set of data for the same subjects along the other axis. By mapping a coordinate for each individual along the x and y axes, you will soon have a set of dots. The more closely that set of dots forms a line, the more of a discernible correlation you have.

Figure 11-19 uses a scatterplot to show the distribution of Texas public libraries serving between 10,000 and 20,000 persons by income and circulation per capita in 1993.

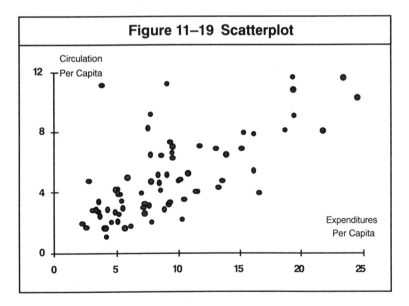

The plots displayed form a clearly discernible pattern that goes from the lower left to the upper right. Because of this, we might be tempted to conclude that a causal relationship exists between expenditures per capita and circulation per capita—that is, the more a library spends, the greater its circulation. But remember the pitfall of correlation analysis: the presence of correlation does not necessarily indicate a causal relationship between the data.

While we can safely say that for these libraries there is a correlation between income and circulation, we cannot safely say that greater expenditure causes higher circulation. Certainly we would like to say this, but the truth could be that both of these trends are driven by a common factor or set of factors. For example, it could well be that the more affluent towns tend to be or the higher the level of educational attainment, the greater value the community places on the library, which causes both the greater level of support *and* the greater interest in the library. All the same, scatterplots can provide some interesting displays, revealing correlation where you did not expect it. And scatterplots allow us to see the correlations where they would be much harder to discover by simply looking at a table of numbers.

If your software is sufficiently advanced, you may also be able to create three-dimensional plots, so that instead of only the vertical y and horizontal x axes, you will also plot a third set of variables along a line that seems to move from back to front called the z-axis. In contrast to the 3-D bar and pie chart displays considered above, three-dimensional scatterplots are a useful form of graphic display. In fact, they are often the only way to demonstrate the correlation of three values simultaneously—a technique that is of great importance to scientists, demographers, economists, and other social scientists. For the purpose of descriptive library statistics at the local level, however, it is very unlikely that you will ever have to use even a two-dimensional scatterplot, much less one that is three-dimensional. If you do, you can refer to one of the works cited in the bibliography.

MAPS

Maps are a form of graphic display that you may very well want to use. The rise of the concept of geographical information system (GIS) software in the last few years has made possible a level of geographical analysis that previously could have been done only with tedious effort. A number of commercial software packages are now available that can create geographic display and analysis of huge amounts of data.

These software packages can produce maps from national-level data down to specific neighborhoods. Figure 11-20 is a map that was produced by E. Walter Terrie, a demographer at the University of Florida. This display maps the location of every administrative entity in the contiguous forty-eight states. Each dot

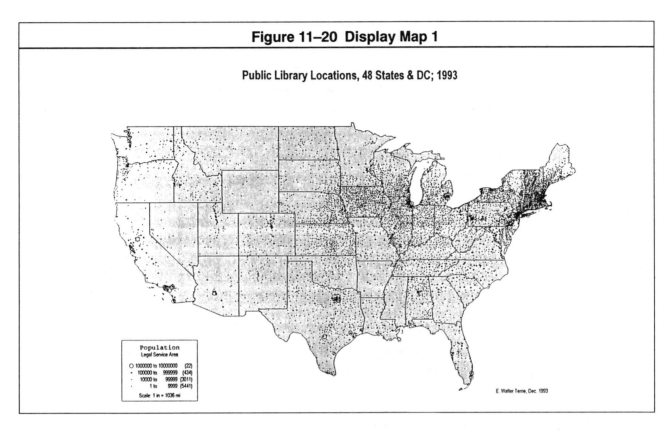

Figure 11–20 Display Map 1

Public Library Locations, 48 States & DC; 1993

represents the center point (or centroid) of the zip code area of the street address of the administrative entity. Dr. Terrie has been closely involved with the FSCS public library data collection effort for many years, and this map was created from data found in the public library universe file discussed in Chapter 2.

The map of Kentucky (Figure 11-21) was produced by Jay Bank at the Kentucky State Library and shows expenditures per capita for each county in the state.

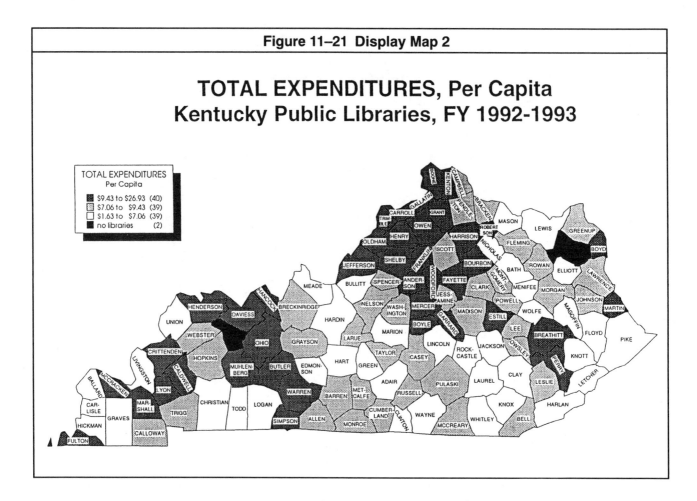

Figure 11–21 Display Map 2

Finally, the map in Figure 11-22 was produced by Christie M. Koontz, an expert in the use of GIS software for library planning purposes. This map shows the branch locations of the Jacksonville (Florida) Public Library in relation to census tracts where African American residents account for more than 50% of the population. This micropresentation differs dramatically from Walt Terrie's presentation above and demonstrates the extreme level of localization that can be achieved with a "high-end" software package.

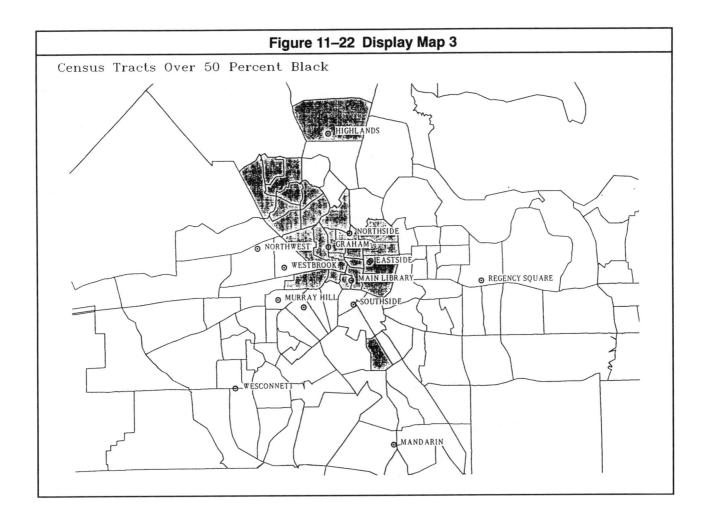

Figure 11–22 Display Map 3

Census Tracts Over 50 Percent Black

While many library researchers have used GIS applications to create descriptive pictures of the status of library service, Koontz's work has brought market-based principles to the library applications of GIS. Most notably, these applications include population, transportation, economic, and demographic analyses that can be used for such purposes as the placement of new library branches and the development of services responsive to community needs.

While maps can be extremely useful, you will confront several hurdles on your way to producing high-quality maps. First, you will need the software. There is a tremendous range in price, from products that start at less than a thousand dollars to top-line products that cost several thousand dollars.

Buying the software is only the beginning. Before you can create maps, you will need something called *boundary files*. These are the files that tell the computer how to interpret the data and draw the maps. Boundary files come in a variety of formats, some of which are published by the U.S. government. Be sure to ask when you are buying your software what, if any, boundary files are included and what format files the program uses.

Finally, once you have the software and boundary files, learning to use especially the more sophisticated programs can be challenging. These are highly complex programs that will probably require a significant investment of time in loading, formatting, interpreting, and refining the presentation. When selecting software, try to use it before you buy it to get a feel for the ease or difficulty of use.

Mapping software can be a valuable tool, especially in larger urban libraries with multiple outlets and diverse communities. For these reasons, GIS is a growing area of interest not just in library work, but also for many fields within the social sciences, education, business, and government.

PRINCIPLES OF VISUAL DISPLAYS

At the end of Chapter 9 we discussed some principles of responsible and effective data use, such as using relevant and accurate figures and looking for analytical rather than merely descriptive uses of data. These principles apply to graphic representations of data, but there are a couple of other principles that apply to charting as well. Tufte says that one should "allow cognitive principles to drive visual principles" ("Presenting Data"). What he means is that you should think about how the viewer will approach and consider the data you are trying to represent. He also means that the way we think should inform the way we create graphs. Find the presentation that is most compatible with the subject matter. If you are demonstrating geographic data, use a map. If you are showing only two dimensions of data, use a two-dimensional presentation, and save the 3-D chart for data that have three dimensions.

Another principle of good graphic use is to give the viewer the full picture. Never show a chart all by itself. Put the chart in the context of enough tabular and narrative data that viewers can be satisfied that there is not data hidden from them and that the graph is an accurate representation of the truth. If you are showing figures against a base year, show the base year figures so the viewer will understand the full picture.

A third principle—one I touched on before—is to make it as easy as possible for the viewer to see what is going on. This means simultaneously weeding out distracting and superfluous elements and simplifying what remains. Your goal is to create the least amount of work for the viewer by making it easy to see the relationships that are most important between various visual elements of your presentation. Whenever possible, put your labels directly on the chart elements rather than boxing them in a separate legend. Point out significant elements directly on the chart, as we did above in our bar chart showing the start of the summer reading program. At the same time, root out all unnecessary elements on your charts. Do you really need that grid behind the bars? Do all those tick marks on the y-axis add information? Why do all the bars have to be shaded? Can you do with fewer numerical increments along the axes? Strive to make your charts as simple and straightforward as possible.

Finally, your work with charts and graphs will be helped tremendously if you start a file of best uses. While library data uses will be important to locate and use, you should collect liberally from other areas as well. Keep an eye out for graphics in newspapers, magazines, newsletters, and books—even on television. Save whatever you can in a folder so that when it comes time to create your presentation, you can learn from others' work with graphics. The best elements of data design are old and time-honored. It is not necessary to start from scratch every time you build a new presentation.

12 FUTURE TRENDS IN LIBRARY STATISTICS

Obviously, the measurement and evaluation of public library programs do not exist in a vacuum. They are integrally involved with the tide of professional interest, professional preoccupations, and the changing role libraries play—or that we would have them play—in society.

Over the last twenty years, the nature of public library statistical collection has changed dramatically. The rise of output measures is a significant development in this regard, since it has radically altered how we measure what we do. Within the last five years, we have seen a huge increase in interest in measuring services to children. Thus, in 1992, *Output Measures for Public Library Services to Children* (Walter) joined *Planning and Role-Setting for Public Libraries* (McClure et al.) and *Output Measures for Public Libraries* (Van House et al.). *Output Measures and More: Planning and Evaluating Public Library Services to Young Adults* (Walter) further extended this coverage in 1995.

But has the rise in importance of these ideas been the cause or the result of a change in our professional interests and preoccupations? During these same years, the nature of the public library has changed as well. The rise of interest in output measures has mirrored our growing interest in the role of the public library in the community, in reaching out to the previously underserved, in taking on social service roles (such as literacy tutoring and information and referral), and in making library services more responsive to the needs of our current and potential users. Similarly, the rise of interest in output measures for children's services has followed a widespread recognition of the important role of the public library in the intellectual development of children, especially preschool children. As the public library began to acquire new roles in the 1970s and 1980s, we found new ways to measure our effectiveness in filling those roles. Professionally, we now regard the public library as a blend of educational institution, social service agency, and recreational facility. These roles are reflected in our statistical measures.

You don't really need a crystal ball to see what the future holds. You need only look at the areas of greatest interest to the profession. There seem to be three key areas that should be briefly explored: the increasing reliance on Internet and other electronic resources in our libraries; the contribution of the library to the economic well-being of the community; and the new, largely unexplored area of outcome measures.

THE INTERNET AND ELECTRONIC RESOURCES

In the last four years, the Internet has become one of the central preoccupations of the library profession. We have become obsessed with the significance of this tool for our libraries. A number of states have begun to link all their libraries to the Internet. Electronically networked information carries a combined promise and threat to alter radically our collections, our staffing, our expenditures, and how we deliver services to the public.

There is a growing recognition that the things we are now measuring will become increasingly irrelevant and that we have barely begun to measure those aspects of our work which will become of tremendous significance over the next several years. Collections are a very nice illustration of this point. Materials are being transferred to electronic formats at a dizzying rate, especially in the areas of periodicals, reference resources, government information, and even literary classics. Library access to these materials on-line has likely increased dramatically, but because we measure only the size of the print collection, we are not capturing this. What's more, in the discussion of materials ownership versus materials access, can libraries even be said to "own" these materials? No, but they are available to patrons, so our traditional measure of the size of the collection may soon no longer fully indicate the true extent of resources available to the public.

In the coming months and years, we will see an increasing emphasis on data collection in these new areas of electronic access, the Internet, document delivery, and so forth.

THE MARKET ANALYSIS OF LIBRARY SERVICE

Another area that is gaining interest is the concept of libraries as an integral component of the economic fabric of the community. This idea cuts two ways, leading to some data collection and analysis concerns.

The first area of interest is in proving that libraries contribute to local economic development. This can occur in a number of ways, including providing informational resources needed to support the growth of business. Another way is that libraries contribute to the quality of life, thus making the community more attractive to a talented and well-educated employment base. Still another way is that libraries contribute to an expanded culture of educational opportunities in the community in a way that encourages the positive growth of young people and decreases the risk of drug abuse, crime, vandalism, and other undesirable and costly problems.

The other broad area of interest is in running the library according to marketing principles. According to this theory, libraries are in every way retailers of services, even though the consumers pay for those services through their taxes rather than directly. This theory applies a whole new set of analytical measures that might seem very different and possibly even alien to library work: unit costs, product development, advertising, market penetration, market analysis, and so forth. The benefit of this approach, say proponents, is that library managers can begin to think objectively about their services, focusing on the bottom lines of use, demand, cost-effectiveness, and productivity. This idea is gaining momentum and is attractive because it enables the library—in this era of private-sector downsizing and public-sector scrutiny—to demonstrate the exact ways it contributes to the economic development of the community, and that it is efficiently run and managed according to principles and standards common in the private sector.

And all this is fine, but it requires numbers. It is easy to see that such a management approach would be very interested in and dependent upon quantifiable data to support its arguments. Some libraries have done better than others in this regard. A number of articles in the *Bottom Line* and other library journals have suggested a variety of measures of the economic value of public libraries, but measuring library work in this way seems to have several difficulties. Because public libraries are basically run in a not-for-profit mode, some of the data proposed to support the analysis seem to have an almost metaphorical quality.

Nevertheless, for many in the profession, this type of analysis is very attractive and has been effective in maintaining and increasing funding for some libraries. Further, the ability to demonstrate that libraries enhance the economic life of the community would be highly desirable. As these ideas grow in prominence—as they very well may—standardized measures will be developed to prove the positive impact of libraries in the local economy. At the same time, creative new measures of program effectiveness, resource allocation, and service delivery may develop out of this philosophy.

OUTCOME MEASURES

The buzzword of the 1990s in the area of evaluation is "outcomes." Outcomes may seem at first glance the same as outputs, but they are really very different. Outputs measure volume, usage, and quality of service. They are easily measurable and quantifiable. They describe how many, how much, and how well.

Outcomes are an attempt to take the assessment one step further. Outcomes describe the impact of the service on people's lives. How was the patron's life enhanced by using the public library and its service? This is the big question that outcomes would attempt to address.

Examples of outcome measures might be: How many people found jobs because of the library's resources? How many people achieved the literacy skills needed to function effectively in society? How did use of the public library help children improve their school performance?

While everyone might agree that these are just the kind of questions we would like to answer about our libraries, it is not so easy to decide what the appropriate measures would be, and more significantly, how to capture them. Outcome measures are beyond the types of data collection methods discussed throughout this book. Outcome measures move us into an area where results are largely dependent upon information that would, at best, be difficult to collect. They also raise a daunting question of definitions. Because such definitions rest on qualitative terms, clarity becomes far more difficult to achieve. Outcomes would seem to lend themselves to anecdotal demonstrations of effectiveness, but how can that anecdotal evidence be made meaningful on anything beyond a local library level?

Outcomes are very popular among our funding authorities. Politicians like outcomes because they show the human benefits of public funding more eloquently than cold statistics can. So while outcomes will likely not be introduced at the federal or state levels (where, ironically, they have generated the greatest interest), we as a profession should continue to define a standard set of outcome measures and means to collect them. After all, the best possible measure of our public libraries would assess the difference they make in people's lives.

APPENDIX A: SAMPLE FORMS FOR DATA COLLECTION

The form in Figure A-1 could be used to create a daily log of library activities in a small or medium-sized library without an automated circulation system. Data collected in this way provide a huge amount of information about patterns of use, which days are most busy, correlations between library activities, use of the collection by material type, and more.

Figure A–1   Daily Statistics

Date: _____

Visits:

Total:_____

Program Attendance:

Total:_____

Circulation:

Adult	Juvenile
Books:	
Videos:	
Cassettes:	
Magazines:	
Other:	
Total:	

Reference:

Total:_____

Cash Receipts:

Fines:	
Copy Machine:	
Donations:	
Lost cards:	
Lost items:	
Damaged items:	
Other:	
Total:	

Nonautomated libraries can use a form like Figure A-2 to track daily circulation for an entire month in several formats and materials classes. The form is similar to ones found in circulation logbooks sold by commercial library supply companies. The logbook is preferable to loose pages since it binds forms together in a single book and contains forms to total circulation statistics annually.

Figure A–2   Daily Circulation

Month: _____ 19____

DAILY CIRCULATION

Date	Books Adult	Books Juvenile	Videos	CDs	Magazines	Total
1						
2						
3						
4						
5						
6						
7						
8						
9						
10						
11						
12						
13						
14						
15						
16						
17						
18						
19						
20						
21						
22						
23						
24						
25						
26						
27						
28						
29						
30						
31						
Totals						

The form in Figure A-3 logs library visits each hour of the week, then allows for daily totals for each column. These data can be of tremendous value in developing a detailed picture of patterns of library use. This form could just as easily be used to count reference transactions or any other kind of constantly occurring library activity. A form of this type is not incompatible with automated counting devices. Staff could take the hourly count from the meter on such a device so that they did not have to mark each person entering the building.

Figure A–3 Library Visits

	Monday	Tuesday	Wednesday	Thursday	Friday	Saturday	Sunday
9-10							
10-11							
11-12							
12-1							
1-2							
2-3							
3-4							
4-5							
5-6							
6-7							
7-8							
8-9							
Totals							

A form such as Figure A-4 could be used to record items received at the library. The form records in a variety of formats and material classes. A form of this type can be kept for each month or for longer or shorter periods depending on the recording needs of the library.

		BOOKS				NON-PRINT MATERIALS				
Date	Adult Fiction	Adult Non-fic	Juv	Juv Non-fic	Audio	Videos	Micro-forms	Other	TITLES	VOLUMES
TOTAL										

Figure A–4   Items Received

This form (Figure A-5) provides a detailed record of each reference question received and would provide a wealth of information about the reference function, including search patterns, time of receipt and response, success rate, effectiveness of the collection to meet demand, subject areas of highest demand, and percentage of questions answered and referred.

Figure A–5 Reference Request Form

Date:_____   Time: _____

Patron name: _____

Phone_____   Fax:_____   E-mail:_____

Question:_____

_____

_____

_____

_____

Date needed by: _____

Sources checked: _____

_____

_____

Answer	Source
Request referred to **Phone:** _____	**Follow-up status**
Staff (initials)	**Date completed**

This reference log (Figure A-6) is somewhat simpler than the transaction record form, but will nevertheless yield valuable information about reference services.

Figure A–6 Reference Log					
Date	**Question**	**Date Answered**	**Date Referred**	**Agency**	**Staff Initials**

A volunteer log (Figure A-7) is an unobtrusive way to obtain information on your volunteers. The form contains a row for staff to tally the number of hours worked by volunteers. This information may be required by your state library and will be of value in recognizing your volunteers.

Figure A–7   Volunteer Log

(Volunteers, for our records please log in the time you arrived and time leaving. *Thank you!*)

Date	Name	Time IN	Time OUT	# hours for staff use

Figure A-8 is an example of a worksheet form used to create a record of collection sampling for various situations. Not all samples need be this thorough, but a full sampling of a short range of cards—while time-consuming—would provide a great deal of information about the collection.

Figure A–8   Collection Sample Worksheet

First call no. in range checked:	Last call no. in range:
Title:	Title:

Number of inches in shelf list:
Number of cards in shelf list:
Of range sampled, how many in shelflist were NOT in OPAC?
How many were shown in OPAC as on shelf, but were actually checked out?
How many were shown in OPAC, but unaccounted for in circ or other records?
How many of the sample were in circulation?
Notes:

Staff:	Date:

The form in Figure A-9 is sufficient for a two-week sample of in-house use in the same part of the library. In a smaller library, this form can be used for the entire library. Staff would tally hash marks for each of several classes of materials with totals for the row (total daily in-library use) and column (total for the material type). This form will allow analysis of the data by day of the week, material type, and, if collected in different parts of the library, of relative uses between departments.

Figure A–9   In-Library Materials Use

Area/Department: _____

Date/Time	Books	Newspapers	Magazines	Other	Total
Totals:					

APPENDIX B: SELECTED FSCS/NCES DEFINITIONS

The following are key definitions used in the Federal State Cooperative System (FSCS) for Public Library Data as published in 1995 by the National Center for Education Statistics (NCES) and the U.S. National Commission on Libraries and Information Science (NCLIS). The definitions form the basis for state data collection of these items and are widely reproduced in state library annual report instructions to local public libraries.

Public Library

A public library is established under state enabling laws or regulations to serve the residents of a community, district, or region. A public library is an entity that provides at least the following: 1) an organized collection of printed or other library materials, or a combination thereof; 2) a paid staff to provide and interpret such materials as required to meet the informational, cultural, recreational, and/or educational needs of a clientele; 3) an established schedule in which services of the staff are available to clientele; and 4) the facilities necessary to support such a collection, staff, and schedule.

Note: State law determines whether an entity is a public library.

Administrative Entity

This is the public library, state library agency, system, federation, or cooperative service that is legally established under local or state law to provide public library service to a particular client group (for example, the population of a local jurisdiction, the population of a state, or the public libraries located in a particular region). The Administrative Entity may be administrative only and have no outlets, it may have a single outlet, or it may have more than one outlet.

Name	This is the legal name of the Administrative Entity.
	Note: Provide the name of the public library. If the Administrative Entity is a state library agency or a system, federation, or cooperative service, provide its name.
Street Address	This is the complete street address of the Administrative Entity.
	Note: Do not report a post office box or general delivery.
City	This is the city or town in which the Administrative Entity is located.
County of the Entity	This is the county in which the Administrative Entity is located.
Zip1	This is the standard five-digit postal zip code for the street address of the Administrative Entity.
Zip2	This is the four-digit postal zip code extension for the street address of the Administrative Entity.
Phone	This is the telephone number of the Administrative Entity, including area code.
Number of Branch Libraries	A branch library is an auxiliary unit of an Administrative Entity which has at least all of the following: 1) separate quarters; 2) an organized collection of library materials; 3) paid staff; and 4) regularly scheduled hours for being open to the public.
Number of Bookmobiles	A bookmobile is a traveling branch library. It consists of at least all of the following: 1) a truck or van that carries an organized collection of library materials; 2) paid staff; and 3) regularly scheduled hours (bookmobile stops) for being open to the public.

PAID STAFF

Report figures as of the last day of the fiscal year. Include all positions funded in the library's budget whether those positions are filled or not. To ensure comparable data, 40 hours per week has been set as the measure of full-time employment (FTE).

ALA-MLS

Librarians with master's degrees from programs of library and information studies accredited by the American Library Association.

Total Librarians

Persons with the title of librarian who do paid work that usually requires professional training and skill in the theoretical or scientific aspects of library work, or both, as distinct from its mechanical or clerical aspect. This data element also includes ALA-MLS.

OPERATING INCOME

Report income used for operating expenditures as defined below. Include federal, state, or other grants. DO NOT include income for major capital expenditures, contributions to endowments, income passed through to another agency (e.g., fines), or funds unspent in the previous fiscal year. (Funds transferred from one public library to another public library should be reported by only one of the public libraries. The State Data Coordinator shall determine which library will report these funds.)

Local Government

This includes all tax and non-tax receipts designated by the community, district, or region and available for expenditure by the public library. Do not include the value of any contributed or in-kind services or the value of any gifts and donations, fines, or fees.

State Government

These are all funds distributed to public libraries by State government for expenditure by the public libraries, except for federal money distributed by the State. This includes funds from such sources as penal fines, license fees, and mineral rights.

Federal Government This includes all federal government funds distributed to public libraries for expenditure by the public libraries, including federal money distributed by the State.

Other Income This is all income other than that reported in . . . [local, state and federal government income]. Include, for example, monetary gifts and donations received in the current year, interest, library fines, and fees for library services. Do not include the value of any contributed or in-kind services or the value of any nonmonetary gifts and donations.

OPERATING EXPENDITURES Operating expenditures are the current and recurrent costs necessary to support the provision of library services.

Salaries and Wages Expenditures This includes salaries and wages for all library staff (including plant operations, security, and maintenance staff) for the fiscal year. Include salaries and wages before deductions but exclude employee benefits.

Employee Benefits These are the benefits outside of salaries and wages paid and accruing to employees (including plant operations, security, and maintenance staff), regardless of whether the benefits or equivalent cash options are available to all employees. Include amounts spent by the reporting unit for direct, paid employee benefits including Social Security, retirement, medical insurance, life insurance, guaranteed disability income protection, unemployment compensation, workmen's compensation, tuition, and housing benefits. Only that part of any employee benefits paid out of the public library budget should be reported.

Collection Expenditures	This includes all expenditures for materials purchased or leased for use by the public. It includes print materials, microforms, machine-readable materials, audiovisual materials, etc.
Other Operating Expenditures	This includes all expenditures other than those for staff and collection.

Note: Include expenses such as binding, supplies, repair or replacement of existing furnishings and equipment, and costs incurred in the operation and maintenance of physical facilities.

Capital Outlay	These are funds for the acquisition of or additions to fixed assets such as building sites, new buildings and building additions, new equipment, initial book stock, furnishings for new or expanded buildings, and new vehicles. This excludes replacement and repair of existing furnishings and equipment, regular purchase of library materials, and investments for capital appreciation.

Note: Local accounting practices shall determine whether a specific item is a capital expense or an operating expense regardless of the examples in this definition.

LIBRARY COLLECTION	Report physical units. For smaller libraries when volume data are not available, title information may be substituted. Items which are packaged together as a unit, e.g., two compact discs, two films, or two video cassettes, and are generally checked out as a unit, should be counted as *one* physical unit.
Book/Serial Volumes	Books are non-periodical printed publications bound in hard or soft covers, or in loose-leaf format. Serials are publications issued in successive parts, usually at regular intervals, and as a rule, intended to be

continued indefinitely. Serials include periodicals (magazines), newspapers, annuals (reports, yearbooks, etc.), memoirs, proceedings, and transactions of societies. Except for the current volume, count unbound serials as a volume when the library has at least half of the issues in a publisher's volume.

Audio

These are materials on which sounds (only) are stored (recorded) and that can be reproduced (played back) mechanically or electronically, or both. Included are records, audiocassettes, audio cartridges, audiodiscs, audioreels, talking books, and other sound recordings.

Film

The term film is used interchangeably with "motion picture" which is a length of film, with or without recorded sound, bearing a sequence of still images that creates the illusion of movement when projected in rapid succession (usually 18 or 24 frames per second). Motion pictures are produced in a variety of sizes (8, super 8, 16, 35, 55, and 70 mm) and in a variety of forms (cartridge, cassette, loop, and reel).

Video

These are materials on which pictures are recorded, with or without sound. Electronic playback reproduces pictures, with or without sound, using a television receiver or monitor.

Subscriptions

This refers to the arrangements by which, in return for a sum paid in advance, periodicals, newspapers, or other serials are provided for a specified number of issues.

Note: Count subscriptions purchased from the library's budget and those donated to the library as gifts. Count titles, including duplicates, not individual issues. Include the total number of subscriptions for all outlets.

SERVICES

Public Service Hours/Year

This is the sum of annual public service hours for outlets.

Note: Include the hours open for public service for centrals, branches, bookmobiles, and books-by-mail only. For each bookmobile, count only the hours during which the bookmobile is open to the public. For Administrative Entities that offer ONLY books-by-mail service, count the hours that the outlet is staffed for service. Minor variations in scheduled public service hours need not be included, however extensive hours closed to the public due to natural disasters or other events should be excluded even if the staff is scheduled to work.

Library Visits

This is the total number of persons entering the library for whatever purposes during the year.

Note: If an actual count of visits is unavailable, determine an annual estimate by counting visits during a typical week in October and multiplying the count by 52. A "typical week" is a time that is neither unusually busy or unusually slow. Avoid holiday times, vacation periods for key staff, or days when unusual events are taking place in the community or the library. Choose a week in which the library is open its regular hours. Include seven consecutive calendar days, from Sunday through Saturday (or whenever the library is usually open).

Reference Transactions

A reference transaction is an information contact which involves the knowledge, use, recommendations, interpretation, or instruction in the use of one or more information sources by a member of the library staff. It includes information and referral services. Information sources include printed and nonprinted materials, machine-readable databases, catalogs and other holdings records, and, through communication or referral, other libraries and institutions and people inside and outside the library. The request may come in person, by phone, by fax, mail, or by electronic-mail from an adult, a young adult, or child.

Do not count directional transactions or questions of rules or policies. Examples of directional transactions are "Where are the children's books?" and "I'm looking for a book with the call number 811.2G." An example of a question of rules or policies is "Are you open until 9:00 tonight?"

Total Circulation

The total annual circulation of all library materials of all types, including renewals.

Note: Count all materials in all formats that are charged out for use outside the library. Interlibrary loan transactions included are only items borrowed for users. Do not include items checked out to another library.

INTERLIBRARY LOANS

Provided To

These are library materials, or copies of the materials, provided by one library to another upon request. The libraries involved in interlibrary loans are not under the same library administration. These data are reported as annual figures.

Received From

These are library materials, or copies of the materials, received by one library from another library upon request. The libraries involved in interlibrary loans are under the same library administration. These data are reported as annual figures.

Circulation of Children's Materials

The total annual circulation of all children's materials in all formats to all users. It includes renewals.

Children's Program Attendance

The count of the audience at all programs for which the primary audience is children. Includes adults who attend programs intended primarily for children.

Note: *Output Measures for Public Library Service to Children: A Manual for Standardized Procedures* (ALA, 1992) defines children as persons age 14 and under.

BIBLIOGRAPHY

Alley, Brian, and Jennifer Cargill. *Keeping Track of What You Spend: The Librarian's Guide to Simple Bookkeeping.* Phoenix: Oryx Press, 1982.

Baker, Sharon L., and F. Wilfred Lancaster. *The Measurement and Evaluation of Library Services.* 2nd ed. Arlington, VA: Information Resources Press, 1991.

Bank, Jay, comp. and ed. *Statistical Report of Kentucky Public Libraries, Fiscal Year 1993-1994.* Frankfort, KY: Department for Libraries and Archives, Field Services Division, 1995.

Bertin, Jacques. *Semiology of Graphics: Diagrams, Networks, Maps.* Translated by William J. Berg. Madison: University of Wisconsin Press, 1983.

Bowker Annual: Library and Book Trade Almanac. New Providence, NJ: R. R. Bowker.

Chambers, John M., et al. *Graphical Methods for Data Analysis.* Wadsworth Statistics/Probability Series. Belmont, CA: Wadsworth International Group; Boston: Duxbury Press, 1983.

Clark, Philip M. "Putting Your Library on the Map." *Bottom Line* 5 (fall 1991): 38-40.

Cohen, Steven, and Ronald Brand. *Total Quality Management in Government: A Practical Guide for the Real World.* San Francisco: Jossey-Bass Public Administration Series, 1993.

Connor, Jane Gardner. *Children's Library Services Handbook.* Phoenix: Oryx Press, 1990.

Davis, Jinnie Y., and David M. Paynter, eds. *Performance Measures for Libraries.* Special issue of *North Carolina Libraries* 48 (fall 1990): 160-217.

DeProspo, Ernest R., Ellen Altman, and Kenneth E. Beasley, with the assistance of Ellen C. Clark. *Performance Measures for Public Libraries.* Chicago: Public Library Association and American Library Association, 1973.

Dewey, Patrick R. *202+ Software Packages to Use in Your Library: Descriptions, Evaluations, and Practical Advice.* 101 Micro Series. Chicago: American Library Association, 1992.

Dixon, Wilfrid J., and Frank J. Massey, Jr. *Introduction to Statistical Analysis.* 4th ed. New York: McGraw-Hill, 1983.

Estabrook, Leigh Stewart, ed. *Applying Research to Practice: How to Use Data Collection and Research to Improve Library Management Decision Making.* Allerton Park Institute 33. Urbana-Champaign: University of Illinois, Graduate School of Library and Information Science, 1992.

Halstead, Kent. "Library Price Indexes for Colleges and Schools." In: *Bowker Annual: Library and Book Trade Almanac.*

Hernon, Peter. *Statistics for Library Decision Making: A Handbook*. Information Management, Policy, and Services. Norwood, NJ: Ablex Publishing Corporation, 1989.

Hernon, Peter, and Charles R. McClure. *Evaluation and Library Decision Making*. Information Management, Policy, and Services. Norwood, NJ: Ablex Publishing Corporation, 1990.

Huff, Darrell. *How to Lie with Statistics*. New York: W. W. Norton, 1954.

Jurow, Susan, and Susan B. Barnard, eds. *Integrating Total Quality Management in a Library Setting*. New York: Haworth Press, 1993.

Koontz, Christie M. *Library Siting and Location Handbook for Library Managers*. New York: Greenwood, forthcoming.

Lance, Keith Curry, and Katy Sherlock. "Use of Statistics in Management Decisions." In Estabrook 40-51.

Long, Sandi. *Let's Tell Your Story; or, How to Sell Your Library Using Statistics*. Salt Lake City: Utah State Library Division, Department of Community and Economic Development, 1994.

McClure, Charles R., et al. *Planning and Role-Setting for Public Libraries: A Manual of Options and Procedures*. Chicago: American Library Association, 1987.

Menzul, Faina. "Use of Information Service Statistics for Communications with Management." *Bulletin of the American Society for Information Science* 19 (December 1992/January 1993): 21-22.

Morton, Bruce. "Statistical Data as a Management Tool for Reference Managers; or, Roulette by the Numbers." *Reference Librarian* 19 (1987): 87-109.

Mosteller, Frederick. "Classroom and Platform Performance." *American Statistician* 34 (February 1980): 11-17.

Muir, Holly J. "Benchmarking: What Can It Do for Libraries?" *Library Administration and Management* 9 (spring 1995): 103-5.

Peischl, Thomas M. "Benchmarking: A Process for Improvement." *Library Administration and Management* 9 (spring 1995): 99-101.

Public Library Association Statistical Report. Chicago: Public Library Association, [19— annual].

Rubin, Richard. *In-House Use of Materials in Public Libraries*. Urbana: University of Illinois, Graduate School of Library and Information Science, 1986.

Senkevitch, Judith Jamison. "Analyzing Productivity in the Era of Accountability." *Bottom Line* 5 (fall 1991): 25-28.

Smith, Mark. *Counting What You Do: A Guide to Collecting and Reporting Public Library Statistics.* Austin: Texas State Library, 1992.

Terrie, E. Walter. "Counting Public Libraries in the United States." In *Data Comparability and Public Policy: New Interest in Public Library Data: Papers Presented at Meetings of the American Statistical Association.* Working Paper No. 94-07. Washington, DC: U.S. Department of Education, Office of Educational Research and Improvement, National Center for Education Statistics,1994.

Texas Public Library Summary for 1993. Austin: Texas State Library, Library Development Division, 1994.

Tufte, Edward R. *Envisioning Information.* Cheshire, CT: Graphics Press, 1990.

———. "Presenting Data and Information." One-day course, Austin, TX, 30 March 1995.

———. *The Visual Display of Quantitative Information.* Cheshire, CT: Graphics Press, 1983.

U.S. Department of Education. National Center for Education Statistics. *Public Libraries in the United States: 1993.* Washington, DC, 1995.

U.S. Department of Labor. Bureau of Labor Statistics. *CPI Detailed Report.* Washington, DC: Government Printing Office [monthly].

U.S. National Commission on Libraries and Information Science [and the] National Center for Education Statistics. *Decplus User's Guide.* Version 2.1. Washington, DC, 1995.

Van House, Nancy A., et al. *Output Measures for Public Libraries: A Manual of Standardized Procedures.* 2nd ed. Chicago: American Library Association, 1982.

Van House, Nancy A., and Thomas A. Childers. *The Public Library Effectiveness Study: The Complete Report.* Chicago: American Library Association, 1993.

Walter, Virginia A. *Output Measures and More: Planning and Evaluating Public Library Services for Young Adults.* Chicago: American Library Association, 1995.

———. *Output Measures for Public Library Service to Children: A Manual of Standardized Procedures.* Chicago: Association for Library Service to Children, Public Library Association, American Library Association, 1992.

Zipkowitz, Fay. "1993 Placements Up, but Full-Time Jobs Are Scarce." *Library Journal* 119 (15 October 1994): 26-32.

Zweizig, Douglas, and Eleanor Jo Rodger. *Output Measures for Public Libraries.* Chicago: American Library Association, 1982.

INDEX

COLOPHON

Mark Smith is library systems administrator at the Texas State Library in Austin, Texas, where in addition to managing the Texas Library System, he is responsible for collecting and publishing annual statistics for the 500 public libraries in Texas. He is the data coordinator for Texas for the Federal-State Cooperative System for Public Library Data (FSCS) and is a member of the FSCS Steering Committee. Smith is editor of *Texas Public Library Statistics* and author of *Counting What You Do: A Guide to Collecting and Reporting Public Library Statistics*, a manual produced in 1992 by the Texas State Library with funds from the U.S. Department of Education and the U.S. National Commission on Libraries and Information Science. Smith is also editor of *Texas Library Journal* and was previously director of the Plainsboro Free Public Library and the Hillsdale Free Public Library in New Jersey.